A QUEST FOR WINGS
FROM TAIL-GUNNER TO PILOT

Left: *Larry Donnelly, 1943.* Right: *Larry in 1966.*

Composite Wings.

A QUEST FOR WINGS
FROM TAIL-GUNNER TO PILOT

G.L. Donnelly, DFM

TEMPUS

First published 2000

PUBLISHED IN THE UNITED KINGDOM BY:

Tempus Publishing Ltd
The Mill, Brimscombe Port
Stroud, Gloucestershire GL5 2QG

PUBLISHED IN THE UNITED STATES OF AMERICA BY:

Arcadia Publishing Inc.
A division of Tempus Publishing Inc.
2 Cumberland Street
Charleston, SC 29401
1-888-313-2665

Tempus books are available in France, Germany and Belgium
from the following addresses:

Tempus Publishing Group	Tempus Publishing Group	Tempus Publishing Group
21 Avenue de la République	Gustav-Adolf-Straße 3	Place de L'Alma 4/5
37300 Joué-lès-Tours	99084 Erfurt	1200 Brussels
FRANCE	GERMANY	BELGIUM

British Library Cataloguing in Publication Data.
A catalogue record for this book is available from the British Library.

ISBN 0 7524 2014 3

Typesetting and origination by Tempus Publishing.
PRINTED AND BOUND IN GREAT BRITAIN

Contents

Foreword

Following his excellent story of The Whitley Boys, Larry Donnelly has produced another fine book expanding on his life in the Royal Air Force from a very young Regular airman, just before the outbreak of World War Two, to that of a career officer in the post-war period up to the '60s.

It is a remarkable story of military aviation in war and peace seen and experienced by one of the thousands of airmen who *Per Ardua Ad Astra* served their King and Country in those tumultuous days.

The narrative flows so well that I could not put it down and I read the manuscript in just two sessions.

It is well illustrated with all the aircraft types which Larry flew, from a fairly obscure American trainer through a whole 'flypast' of well known Bomber, Coastal and Transport Command aircraft, both piston-engined and jet-powered types.

A particular feature of this work that I liked and which the 'lay' reader would appreciate, is Larry's method of leading the reader into each succeeding chapter by giving an excellent brief summary of the progress of the war at that point of his story.

All in all a refreshing story – not run of the mill stuff! It should certainly find its way onto many a bookshelf.

Brian Gaunt
Yorkshire Air Museum
July 2000

Introduction

While putting together material for this book, I came across the following copy of an amusing essay attributed to a present-day schoolboy:

Why I Want To Be A Pilot

I want to be a pilot when I grow up because it is a fun job and easy to do. That is why there are so many pilots flying today. Pilots don't need much school, they just have to learn numbers so they can read the instruments. I guess they should be able to read road maps so they won't get lost. Pilots should be brave so they won't get scared if it is foggy and they can't see, or if a wing or motor falls off, they should stay calm so they'll know what to do. Pilots have to have good eyesight so they can see through clouds and they can't be afraid of thunder and lightning because they are closer to them than we are. The salary that pilots get is another thing I like. They make more money than they can spend. This is because most people think that plane flying is dangerous except pilots don't because they know how easy it is.

There isn't much I don't like except girls. Girls like pilots and all stewardesses want to marry pilots, so they have to chase them away so they don't bother them.

I hope I don't get airsick because I get carsick and if I got airsick I couldn't be a pilot and then I'd have to work!

Today the opportunities available to this aspiring young birdman to enable him to achieve his ambition, are far greater than those available to similarly oriented youngsters of my generation, during the 1930s. The only avenue open for them to fly, unless they had money to pay for private instruction, was to join the Royal Air Force. Nowadays air-minded youngsters have the opportunity to join the Air Training Corps which serves most schools/areas. The ATC wasn't formed until 1941.

I was one of these aspiring youngsters and from an early age wanted to fly as a pilot with the Royal Air Force. As soon as I left school I pestered my parents to give their permission for me to enlist. Eventually they did and I joined the peacetime Regular Air Force, but my apprenticeship to become a pilot proved to be long, and as it turned out, somewhat dangerous!

At the outbreak of the Second World War, I was serving as WOp/AG with a heavy Bomber Squadron. After surviving tours of active flying operations from 1939 to 1943, I was selected for pilot training and successfully graduated at the beginning of 1945, thus achieving my boyhood ambition to get my coveted pilots' wings.

For the next twenty-one years I flew as pilot with the Royal Air Force. On two occasions during my service I had the privilege of serving with the late Air Vice-Marshal B.P. Young, first when he was a Squadron Leader, and second when he was my Station Commander. He was a South African who had joined the RAF before the war and while training as a flight cadet at the RAF College Cranwell in 1958, wrote the following poem which aptly describes the joy of flying:

Flight
(First published in *Wings of War*, P.B. 'Laddie' Lucas, 1983)

How can they know that joy to be alive
who have not flown?
To loop and spin and climb and dive,
the very sky one's own,
The surge of power while engines race,
The sting of speed
The rude wind's buffet on one's face,
To live indeed,

How can they know the grandeur of the sky,
The earth below
The restless sea and waves that break and die
With ceaseless ebb and flow;
The morning sun on drifting clouds
And rolling downs –
And valleyed mist that shrouds
The chimneyed towns?

So long has puny man to earth been chained
Who now is free,
And with the conquest of the air has gained
A glorious liberty,
How splendid is this gift He gave
On high to roam,
The sun a friend, the earth a slave,
The heavens home.

As the climber is drawn to the mountains and the sailor to the sea, so is the airman to the skies. The ensuing chapters in which I describe my service in the Royal Air Force, during war and peace, serve to affirm this ethos and give me the opportunity of paying tribute to those with whom I served and flew, and whose camaraderie I am privileged to have shared.

One

Fledgling

During the 1930s the British Government, realising that Hitler's rise to power in Germany and his policy of re-armament were indications of the possibility of war, gave priority to the re-arming and expansion of the British Armed Forces. The expansion of the Royal Air Force included the formation of Bomber Command. This commenced in July 1936, and called for an additional 2,500 pilots, 2,000 air-observers, 3,800 wireless-operators and 500 air-gunners.

To air-minded youngsters like myself, whose only opportunity to fly was with the Royal Air Force, this was a heaven-sent opportunity. So, shortly after leaving school I presented myself at the nearest RAF recruiting office and offered my services as a prospective pilot. I was bitterly disappointed to be told I was too young and didn't have the necessary qualifications for pilot training. However, the astute Recruiting Sergeant, who I suspect was on commission for the number of recruits he signed up, noted my keenness and tactfully explained that there were other opportunities for me to fly. If for instance, I enlisted as a wireless operator, my lack of years would be no hindrance as long as I obtained my parents' permission. Also if I elected to join to be trained as a wireless operator I would have the opportunity to remuster as pilot at a later date when I had the necessary qualifications.

I was hooked and pestered my parents until they gave me their permission. Luckily I had an ally in an uncle. He was a civilian Morse Instructor at the RAF Electrical and Wireless School at Cranwell, and guided me through the application procedure. After taking the entrance examination and passing the medical (during which I discovered that coughing didn't always apply to colds and that jabs had nothing to do with boxing), I was accepted for training as a wireless operator and in due course sent to No. 1 Electrical and Wireless School at RAF Cranwell.

On arrival I discovered it was not only the home of the RAF Officer Cadet College but also a busy flying station. This information boosted my hopes of getting into the air in the near future. However, the powers that be had other plans for me.

With the other members of my entry I was quickly absorbed into the technical training syllabus and the strict disciplinary training. Technical instruction included lectures on electrical and wireless theory, instruction in sending and receiving Morse Code, Semaphore (signalling with flags) and Aldis (lamp) signalling.

The disciplinary training encompassed foot drill, arms drill (when we staggered around toting Lee Enfield .303 rifles as big as ourselves), constant medical inspections (to ensure we weren't carrying any horrible civilian germs), kit inspections with all items of kit tagged with the owner's personal number and reported to the Inspecting Officer as 'one on, one for inspection and one in the laundry, Sir'. Also included were parades, colour-hoisting, ceremonial and sick parades when you had to march smartly to sick quarters irrespective of your medical condition!

However, it wasn't all work and no play – every Wednesday we had organised sports and the facilities far exceeded those available to us in civvy street. Despite this strict regime, I took to service life like a duck to water; I was prepared to undergo anything to get involved with flying and aeroplanes as soon as I could. I actually managed to do so quicker than I thought I would and thereby hangs a tale.

On Saturday mornings we took part in an inspection and colour-hoisting parade after which we were marched back to the domestic (barracks) area. We were then detailed in parties to carry out other 'character building exercises', namely 'fatigues' (a droll description) and marched to sections around the station to carry out various tasks. I suspect they saved all the most menial jobs for our benefit an example being peeling spuds in the cookhouse, or cleaning oil drip trays in the hangars.

After three such sessions, my enthusiasm waned. So after the next Saturday parade when we were being marched back to barracks I surreptitiously fell out and made my way to the airfield to watch any flying which might be taking place and (could I be so lucky?) maybe scrounge a flight. When I arrived at the airfield there wasn't much flying taking place, but ground crew were working on the parked aircraft. I got into conversation with a fitter working on a De Havilland Rapide and asked him if he thought there might a chance of getting a flight. To my delight he told me that the aircraft he was working on would be going on an air-test soon and pointed out the Sergeant Pilot who would probably be flying it. I nervously approached the Sergeant and asked if I could go on the air test.

'You're not skiving, are you?'

I crossed my fingers and claimed innocence. I'm sure he didn't believe me but to my great delight and surprise he told me to see the 'Chiefy' (SNCO I/C Flight) and get my name in the Flight Authorisation Book. I was off like a shot, had my name entered in the book and subsequently climbed aboard the DH taking my place in one of the seats in the fuselage.

It wasn't long before the engines were started and we taxied out to the take-off point. As this was my very first flight, I was excited and naturally a bit apprehensive but my apprehension subsided as the aircraft took to the air. The flight only lasted about forty-five minutes, but for me it was a most memorable experience and confirmed that flying could be my true vocation.

Now we come to the poignant part of the tale. After landing I returned to the barracks where I was confronted by our irate Corporal Discip who had noted my absence from the 'fatigues' detail. He demanded an explanation and because I must have been still mentally airborne, I blurted out that I'd been flying. He wasn't impressed and I can still remember his expression as he informed me he was putting me on a 'Fizzer' (the dreaded form 252, charge sheet). Two days later I was wheeled in front of our Officer Commanding, who awarded me seven days CB. For the next seven days I was allowed to leave barracks only to attend lectures and to the dining-hall for meals. I also had to report to the Guardroom three times a day wearing full pack and equipment. As an added bonus I had to carry out fatigues, every evening. Yes, you've guessed it, cleaning greasy pans in the cookhouse. However, in my estimation it was a small price to pay for my first ever flight, though I was a bit puzzled that the infliction of punishment was denoted in Service jargon as an award! Another unfortunate member of our entry also got into hot water around the same time. He was a Canadian who came from Manitoba and in one of his letters home he told his parents that he had been 'awarded' CB (Jankers). A few weeks later they sent him a copy of his local newspaper and one of the headlines read: 'Slim Spratt has only been in the Royal Air Force three months and already he has been Awarded Jankers!'

A few weeks later I got airborne again, but this time it was official. To keep our interest on the boil everyone at the beginning of their service was sent on an Air Experience flight. Ours took place in a lumbering Vickers Valentia twin-engine biplane bomber/transport aircraft. It didn't compare with my flight in the smaller Rapide but I enjoyed it. However; some of my colleagues found they weren't in their element and unfortunately soon parted with their breakfasts.

After that brief flight I had to wait until the final stages of our wireless operating training for my next sortie into the wide blue yonder, but it was worth waiting for. We were detailed to carry out air-to-ground wireless exercises from Westland Wapitis, single-engine biplanes with two open cockpits. Although the Wapiti didn't have the performance or look as good as the newer Hawker Hart, it was in my estimation, more of a 'real' aeroplane than either the Rapide or the lumbering Valentia.

Attired in over-sized Sidcot flying suits which fitted where they touched and parachute harnesses which had the potential to turn us into permanent sopranos, we were anchored into the rear cockpit of the Wapiti by means of a 'monkey' chain – a stout strip of webbing

Wireless Operator 'Sparks' badge.

11

which was attached to the cockpit floor and snap-hooked onto a steel loop on the parachute harness between your legs (another hazard to one's appendages!) Despite these discomforts, this was always how I'd envisaged flying and I recall as I stood in the rear cockpit with the slipstream whipping past me, I was able to fight all my fantasy battles with the 'Red Baron'! After successfully completing this most enjoyable final part of the course I graduated and became a fully fledged wireless operator entitled to wear the 'Sparks' badge on the upper sleeve of my uniform – a very proud moment and the first stage of my quest successfully achieved. Hopefully I was on my way towards my ultimate goal!

We were allocated our postings to various units and I found that I was to join a heavy bomber squadron based at Dishforth, North Yorkshire. On my arrival I discovered that 10 Squadron was equipped with Armstrong Whitworth Whitleys, an aircraft I'd neither seen nor heard of. I must say that when I first saw one I wasn't impressed but I consoled myself with the thought it didn't matter what it looked like as long as it got me to where I was happiest – in the air

I soon settled in on the squadron. I was issued with my own flying kit (Sidcot outer with a 'Teddy-bear' inner) beautiful black leather flying boots, a leather flying helmet and parachute and harness. As an added bonus I was entitled to a shilling a day flying pay.

As a 'sprog' tradesman I was attached to a 'winger' (an experienced wireless operator)

Larry Donnelly beside the tail-turret of a Whitley Mk IV, July 1939.

Air-gunners' pre-war Brass Bullet.

one Johnny Fletcher, known as 'Fletch' in the section, who gave me all the 'gen' on our responsibilities and daily duties as wireless tradesmen. We were allocated aircraft on which we had to carry out daily inspections of all the electrical and wireless equipment. Also we were required to fly as the aircraft wireless-operator whenever it went flying. All wireless operators had also to be qualified air-gunners, so to enable me to qualify I received on the job training. This included learning the theory and practice of all aspects of air-gunnery as well as flying on air-to-sea and air-to-air firing exercises. My training culminated when the squadron was detached to RAF Evanton, on the Moray Firth in July 1939, where it carried out an intensive programme of bombing and air-gunnery. I was in my element during the air-to-air and air-to-sea gunnery sorties firing the VGO (Vickers Gas Operated) single guns from the nose and tail turrets and the twin Brownings from the mid-under turret of the Whitley Mk IV.

At the end of this practice camp period I successfully passed the practical and oral examination and was awarded my air-gunners' badge (a winged brass bullet worn on the uniform sleeve above the 'Sparks' badge). For this extra qualification I was now entitled to an extra sixpence a day gunnery pay.

The Squadron returned to Dishforth on 19 August and on 1 September Hitler's forces invaded Poland. Our squadron received orders to mobilise to war establishment and the station was put on a 'war' footing. On the 3rd September, when Hitler ignored an ultimatum from our Prime Minister to withdraw from Poland, Britain declared war.

I had just managed to complete my training in time, but like most of the other

WOp/AGs in our W/T section I was a 'Fledgling'. I was eighteen years old and had the grand total of thiry-one flying hours in my logbook. During the next few days it was very likely we would be flying over Germany putting our training to the test. We were being thrown in at the deep end.

De Havilland Rapide.

Vickers Valentia.

Westland Wapiti.

Two

The Phoney War

For twenty years preceding the Second World War, fear of the bomber had been great, conjuring up nightmares of mass raids on civilian populations in towns and cities. During the Spanish Civil War, Hitler sent his bombers of the 'Condor Legion' to fly for General Franco. When they attacked the unprotected town of Guernica in Northern Spain, killing approximately 1,600 out of a population of 10,000, the fears appeared to be justified.

Germany invaded Poland on 1 September 1939, precipitating the Second World War and Britain and France were drawn into the conflict. Neither they nor Hitler wanted to escalate the war at that time by an all-out bombing offensive, Hitler hoped for a settlement once he had overrun Poland, while, on the other hand the Allies wanted to localise the conflict.

The outcome was that for the first few months of the war, both sides restricted their bombing to warships and naval bases in order to avoid killing civilians and incurring the inevitable reprisals. As it turned out, they were merely putting off the evil day when all-out bombing would start with all its terrible consequences. This period of restraint lasted from September 1939 to April 1940 and was wryly described as 'The Phoney War'.

Full of youthful bravado we fledglings of the regular Royal Air Force wanted to get cracking and bomb Germany from the word go, not realising what it entailed. When our Whitley squadrons of 4 Group Bomber Command were given the task of night reconnaissance and dropping millions of propaganda leaflets on the main cities of Germany and the Occupied Countries of Poland, Czechoslovakia and Austria, our reaction was predictable – 'You can bet the Germans' won't be bombarding us with "toilet paper" and they won't be firing paper shells at us either.'

The first 'bumph' (leaflet) raid was carried out by aircraft from two of our sister Whitley squadrons (51 and 58) on the first night of the war when they dropped leaflets on Hamburg, Bremen and the Ruhr. They were estimated to be successful but two crash-landed in France, luckily without casualties. Opposition had been negligible.

These leaflet raids (known as 'Nickel' sorties) by the Whitley squadrons, continued during the next seven nights over north-west Germany and the Ruhr from English bases or from advanced bases in France with varying success. Two aircraft failed to return from a raid on the Ruhr on the night of the 8/9 September and another collided with a French aircraft as it landed at a French airfield.

Our crew made its debut on the night of 7th/8th to drop Nickels on the German naval base of Kiel. This was the first time we had flown together as a crew although we had flown with each other at different times previously. On 3 September when war was declared, a squadron 'war' crew had been promulgated listing who would fly together as crews. Our crew was made up as follows: F/O Bickford (1st pilot/captain), P/O Henry (2nd pilot/navigator), AC Fletcher (1st WOp/AG), AC Donnelly (2nd WOp/AG) and LAC Gudgeon (tail-gunner).

On the afternoon of the 7th F/O Bickford informed us we would be 'on' that night, so Johnny Fletcher, Freddie Gudgeon and myself carried out a re-check on the W/T equipment and guns on our aircraft, Whitley Mk IV, K9023.

Along with the other crews detailed for the operation we assembled in the Station Operations room for briefing at 20.00hrs. Before it got under way the pilots and aircrew gathered in separate groups swapping corny and macabre jokes attempting to disguise any apprehension. Eventually briefing commenced. We were given our take-off times, targets, weather, the restrictions on the use of W/T and a forecast from the Intelligence Officer on what we could expect in the way of anti-aircraft opposition. Our ebullient commanding officer, Wing Commander W.E. Staton MC DFC★ gave us a pep-talk to bolster our morale. He had done it all before having been a fighter pilot in the First World War, credited with twenty-five victories.

After briefing we dispersed to our various messes for a pre-flight meal then Fletch, Freddie and myself made our way to K9023 which had been brought from the dispersal area and parked on the hangar apron. Fletch and I inspected the load of leaflets which had been stacked in the fuselage forward of the dustbin ventral gun-turret. It would be our task to off-load the leaflets and Fletch observed we were probably in for a busy night. Not long afterwards we took up our positions, the engines were started and after all checks had been completed satisfactorily we taxied to the take-off point. We then obtained take-off clearance from the flare-path controller and lined up for take-off. The skipper opened the throttles of the two Merlins and the Whitley bumped along the grass rapidly passing the goose-neck flares as the speed increased. Soon we were airborne and climbing away from the airfield on course. The time was 00.55 hours on 8 September 1939 and we were on our way to take part in 10 Squadron's first raid over Germany in the Second World War.

We proceeded on course and soon P/O Henry announced over the intercom we were crossing the coast near Flamborough Head. When we were well out to sea I asked for permission to go aft and test the guns in the mid-under turret. As second WOp/AG this was my responsibility. I scrambled into the turret, lowered it and loaded the twin Brownings, then depressing the guns to point to the sea I cocked them, looked through the sight, slipped off the safety catches and pressed the triggers. The guns blazed away as the tracers and incendiaries curved towards the sea and I watched fascinated as this was the first time I had fired the guns at night. While I was checking my guns, Freddie in the tail tested his single VGO (Vickers Gas Operated) gun.

I retracted and vacated the mid-under turret and joined Fletch who was opening the brown paper packages containing the leaflets and stacking the bundles in readiness for dispatch. When we had them stacked we both returned to the cockpit where Fletch resumed his 'listening' watch on the W/T, while I watched P/O Henry working at his navigation charts. I had time to reflect; here we were flying over the North Sea towards Germany to drop propaganda leaflets over Kiel and wondering what was in store for us when we got there. As an impressionable eighteen-year-old I suppose my imagination ran riot, no doubt influenced by the lurid literature I'd read describing the epic air battles of the First World War. Would we avoid being caught in the searchlights and get through the ack-ack barrage which would probably be protecting the naval base?

I was brought back to reality as P/O Henry announced over the intercom we were approaching the enemy coast. The skipper confirmed this and Henry moved forward to obtain a pinpoint. Although it was dark and we were at altitude we could make out the outline of the German coast and see the lights of the then neutral Denmark away to the north of our track.

After Henry had fixed our position we altered course for Kiel and Fletch and I prepared to go aft to drop the leaflets. Just before we left the cockpit the skipper announced that there were searchlights ahead. Excitedly we craned forward and saw four ghostly white beams probing the night sky – our first sight of the German defences. The skipper commented they were probably searching for the aircraft ahead of us. It was reassuring to see none had been illuminated and that there was no ack-ack fire.

Fletch and I left the cockpit and positioned ourselves to drop as soon as we heard the order. I had stationed myself by the flare chute and as Fletch passed the bundles to me I thrust them down the chute. We were at 18,000 feet and using oxygen. The physical effort was considerable and made no easier by the fact that there was only one oxygen point available, so we had to take turns using it changing over when the non-user looked like flaking out.

We heaved out the bundles as fast as we could and initially everything went according to plan. Freddie in the tail-turret reported that the leaflets were scattering behind us. Then however we had a slight hiccup when the securing rubber band came off a bundle in the chute with the result that we were engulfed in a shower of leaflets as the slipstream blew them back at us. However, we pressed on and completed our task. The few searchlights which seemed to be the only active opposition were easily avoided and failed to illuminate us. As we left the area I think we all heaved a thankful sigh of relief that the opposition hadn't been what we'd anticipated.

Our return flight passed without incident except that we had to land at RAF Manby in Lincolnshire to refuel because of a slight navigation miscalculation. When the news got round that we'd just returned from flying over Germany we were the focus of much admiring attention. Later when we finally got back to base our ground crew 'oppos' were also eager to learn how we'd got on and now we were back safely it was easy to dismiss the raid as a piece of cake.

As we did more leaflet raids and night recces it became obvious that our aircraft and equipment fell far short of wartime requirements. Also to add to our chagrin, the 1939/1940 winter turned out to be one of the worst ever recorded and flying conditions were atrocious. Without suitable navigation aids we groped our way over enemy territory in the dark at extreme altitudes to scatter the dreaded 'bumph'. We had to endure temperatures well below zero and cases of frostbite became the rule rather than the exception. Tail-gunners incarcerated in their turrets were especially vulnerable. Our ground crews also suffered the effects of the appalling weather as they had to work in the open on our aircraft which had been dispersed to the fields away from the warmer hangars to minimise the effects of possible attack. They did the daily inspections and minor repairs in sub-zero temperatures and when spanners slipped from numbed fingers, the air was blue with barrack-room 'vernacular'. However despite their difficulties they maintained the aircraft to a high degree of serviceability and deserved the highest praise.

The Nickel raids continued, and on the night of 1/2 October four 10 Squadron's crews were detailed to carry out a reconnaissance and drop leaflets on the German capital. This was the first occasion on which RAF aircraft flew over Berlin during the Second World War. The raid was led by our CO, W/Cdr W.E. Staton and despite encountering severe weather en route and difficulties over the target three crews were successful. Unfortunately the fourth failed to return. This was our squadron's first loss and it was deeply felt – so much for leaflet raids being a piece of cake.

Our crew's second raid was on the night of 15/16 October, a night reconnaissance over the Elbe estuary and dropping leaflets over Hamburg. It wasn't our night. We took off on time and once we were safely airborne I went back to load the guns in the mid-under turret while it was still daylight, a much easier task than fumbling in the dark. In the meantime the front turret started spewing oil back over the cockpit windscreen obscuring the pilots' vision, so they decided to return and land back at base. Unfortunately I was still busily engrossed loading the guns and they omitted to warn me of their intentions. When the aircraft touched down, I was still in the turret. The bottom of it was torn off, my feet hit the ground, my flying boots were ripped off and my legs jammed against the bottom edge of the turret. I managed to grab the turret pipe-lines above my head and hold on until the aircraft came to a halt. By this time Freddie in the tail who had seen my flying boots bounce past his turret had raised the alarm. I was pulled from the turret and laid on the grass. The ambulance arrived with the MO on board.

He gave me a cursory examination after which I was strapped onto a stretcher, loaded into the back of a three-ton truck and transported to Catterick Hospital for x-ray. After being x-rayed I was sedated and tucked up in bed. The following day when I surfaced I was informed there were no bones broken and my injuries were only superficial. After a short stay in hospital I was given sick leave which I spent at home where I attempted to reassure my parents that my injury wasn't the result of doing anything dangerous! When my sick leave expired I returned to base where after a few days I was pronounced fit to resume duty.

On the night of 31 October/1 November our crew was detailed to carry out another reconnaissance of the Jade, Weser and Hamburg areas and on this trip we received our baptism of fire. We were caught in the searchlights over Hamburg and the flak batteries did their damnedest to shoot us down. Luckily for us they were off target and the skipper's evasive tactics enabled us to escape unscathed and to return to land safely at base after being airborne for eight and a half hours. This had been my first experience of being held in searchlights and being fired on. At first I suppose I had been naively fascinated as the different coloured missiles hosed up towards us until I realised just how lethal they were, then apprehension took over (an understatement – I was scared witless!)

After we landed, debriefed and fed, it was off to bed, but it took me some time to get to sleep as I relived the past few hours. I was disturbed after a few hours from my post-flight slumber and told to don my best (No. 1) blue and report to Squadron HQ ASAP with the rest of the crew. We naturally protested about losing our well-earned sleep, but on arrival at HQ we had the pleasant surprise of being presented with other crews of the squadron to His Majesty the King who was visiting the Station. During his inspection of the crews our CO, who was with the escorting party, informed His Majesty that only a few hours previously we had been over Hamburg – a proud moment when we came under Royal scrutiny which compensated for any loss of sleep.

As the months went by we Whitley aircrew realised we had a lot to be thankful for. Apart from one or two daylight anti-shipping 'sweeps' over the North Sea our operations took place at night, unlike the Wellington, Hampden and Blenheim squadrons, who were, in the misguided opinion of the top brass, deemed capable of penetrating the German fighter and flak defences in daylight. During these raids against German fleet targets, they suffered appalling losses from German fighter attacks. By the beginning of 1940 the Wellington and Hampden squadrons were withdrawn from daylight operations but the unfortunate Blenheim crews had to soldier on. The Whitley squadrons also suffered casualties but they were the result of flak or mechanical failure, because at that time the German night-fighter force was at the embryo stage, as was ours. The casualties we did suffer however were a sharp reminder to the young lions on the squadrons that war was more than a big heroic adventure.

In December '39 crew changes took place on our squadron. The tradesmen flying as tail-gunners (fitters/riggers etc.) were taken off flying and replaced by the 2nd WOp/AGs. I took Freddie's place on our crew and ended up as 'tail-end Charlie'. Also, newly trained Sergeant Observers were absorbed into the crews to take over the navigation duties from the 2nd pilots who continued doing the bomb-aiming. Our new Sergeant Observer was

New Air-gunners' badge.

Arthur Knapper whose first trip with us was a daylight anti-shipping sortie just off the German coast – an auspicious start to his operational career!

At the end of December it was announced that all qualified air-gunners were to be awarded a new flying badge to replace the winged bullet. The new badge was half-wing brevet but with the letters AG in the centre. The new badge got a mixed reception – especially from some of the 'old sweat' air-gunners who preferred the brass bullet.

We had a respite from the bumph raids when we were given the task of carrying out 'security patrols' over the German mine-laying seaplane bases in the Frisian Islands, during which flare-paths were bombed and strafed from low level, thus preventing the seaplanes from taking off. This, in our opinion was a much more rewarding task than distributing 'bog paper'! Our efforts were successful, forcing the Germans to transfer the mine-laying task to land-based aircraft on the German mainland. We also carried out offensive patrols over the North Sea to search for and attack German naval and merchant shipping. These searches were in daylight and sometimes took us well within range of the German fighters, but we were fortunate and suffered no interceptions or casualties.

Early in 1940, bumph raids were resumed and extended to include targets as far away as Poland, Czechoslovakia and Austria. Operating from advanced bases in France we carried out raids over Poznan, Vienna and Warsaw. These long-range raids extended the Whitley to its maximum radius of action and could cause problems, especially with the atrocious weather conditions and the lack of navigational aids. Fortunately the opposition was light and in some cases non-existent. One crew on return from a sortie to Vienna reported that when they reached the city blackout precautions were being ignored. The area was a mass of twinkling lights which were being reflected from the black waters of the River Danube. Another crew, after flying blind for some hours on return became uncertain of their position. As dawn broke their fuel stock was getting low. They were pretty certain that they were now over friendly territory and decided to land to find out exactly where they were, so when they spotted a large field they landed and stopped the engines. As they left the aircraft they were greeted by some of the local peasantry and assuming they were French, attempted to establish communication using their far from fluent French. However when the peasants replied they realised to their horror they had landed in Germany they broke all sprint records getting back to the Whitley. Scrambling aboard, they managed to start both engines, then turning the aircraft into the wind whanged open the throttles. They got airborne as German troops appeared on the scene firing their rifles but luckily their aim was off the mark and the Whitley escaped undamaged. By this time it was daylight which enabled the crew to identify their position and land at a nearby French airfield before their fuel ran out.

Villeneuve, code-named 'Sister', was the French base from which we operated to carry out these long-range raids. It was in the champagne producing district and champagne was on sale for only 14 francs a bottle. As the rate of exchange was 172 francs to the pound sterling even we lower-paid ranks could afford to try and emulate the champagne Charlies!

On 1 March 1940, our crew made its first raid on Berlin to drop leaflets on the German capital. I was in the tail turret and it was a freezing cold night, so to combat the possibility of frostbite I pounded my feet up and down on the floor of my tail-turret. As I did so it struck me that having to go to Berlin might be bad enough but having to walk there was a bit much! When we arrived over Berlin the defences had a go at us as we dropped the bumph so although we were at altitude, I gave them a long burst from my VGO, hoping I would hit something. I realised it was unlikely but it gave me some personal satisfaction and some small consolation for the discomfort I was enduring in my draughty turret. We got away unscathed and returned to base safely after a flight lasting ten hours.

On 16 March 1940, the Germans bombed our naval base at Scapa Flow in the Orkneys. During the raid a civilian was killed, so a retaliatory raid was mounted against the German seaplane base at Hornum over which we had previously carried out security patrols. Thirty Whitleys and twenty Hampdens were assigned the task and the raid took place on the night of 19/20 March. This was the first RAF bombing raid on a German land target and needless to say we crews taking part welcomed the prospect of dropping bombs instead of paper. We encountered opposition over the target, but bombed as briefed. As tail-gunner I had a grandstand view after we'd left the target. Only one Whitley was shot down from the squadron with whom we shared our base. The day after the raid we were filmed by British Movietone Newsreel and I was photographed by the national press. Shortly afterwards I went on leave during which I took my girlfriend to a cinema in the nearby town. The programme included a newsreel showing some of the important events of the week. One of them featured our raid over Sylt. Four tail-gunners (including myself) were interviewed. The effect on my girlfriend was electric, she called out excitedly, 'That's you!' With her outburst all heads turned in our direction. Afterwards during our bus journey back to our village we were the subject of much whispering and head nodding. Fame at last!

This raid turned out to be a one off and for the rest of the month of March night reconnaissance and leaflet dropping flights were resumed, but at the beginning of April there were indications that the stalemate was coming to an end. This was confirmed when the Germans invaded Denmark and Norway on 9 April. This would bring about the all-out bombing with all its dreadful consequences which would last until the end of the war.

The so-called Phoney War was over and so was our on the job training. From now on it was 'no holds barred' and the air war would become much grimmer than we had envisaged. However the much maligned bumph raids had at least given us the opportunity to gain experience in operating on long-range raids over enemy territory in adverse weather conditions at night, as well as introducing us to what we could expect from the German anti-aircraft defences. Additionally we were able to suggest improvements to our equipment and technique and to eliminate snags which had come to light. The tempo of raids during the Phoney War was far from hectic, during the period September 1939 to March 1940, I participated in only ten sorties but in the following months that was to change drastically. By the end of September 1940 my total of raids would have reached forty-three.

Three
Norwegian Nightmare

On 4 April 1940 a Blenheim carrying out a daylight reconnaissance over the Elbe Estuary reported that a large number of ships and units of the German fleet were moving northwards in the Schillig Roads. A force of Blenheims was sent to attack the fleet but failed to achieve any results. Another force was sent the next morning but this was aborted due to adverse weather conditions. On the 6th another reconnaissance flight discovered elements of the German fleet at Wilhelmshaven.

Whitley aircraft of 4 Group were dispatched on the night of 6/7 April to reconnoitre north-west Germany and the Ruhr. On return the crews reported large columns of motor transport on the Hamburg to Lubeck roads and at Eckenforde near the port of Kiel a major loading operation was in progress.

During daylight of the 7th, a Blenheim squadron on armed reconnaissance sighted units of the German Fleet made up of destroyers and a cruiser believed to be the *Scharnhorst* or the *Gneisnau*. The Blenheims attacked without effect. A squadron of Wellingtons was sent out immediately but failed to find the enemy ships. A second attempt the following day was also unsuccessful.

It became increasingly evident that something major was afoot and the Krauts were up to no good. This was proved to be correct when on the morning of the 9th, Denmark and Norway were invaded. By the end of the day Denmark was overrun and most of the southern ports and airfields in Norway had been captured. The Germans were now able to carry out air attacks against our Home Fleet already at sea. One destroyer was sunk and three cruisers damaged. These attacks prevented the Home Fleet from taking any offensive action against the German warships at Bergen, so a squadron of Wellingtons and another of Hampdens carried out an attack, claiming hits on a cruiser, the *Konigsberg*, which was finished off on the 10th by Fleet Air Arm Skuas operating from the Orkneys.

The Germans had also captured the airfields at Sola (Stavanger), Fornebu, Kjeller (Oslo) and Vaernes (Trondheim) so were able to control the approaches to the ports of Bergen, Trondheim and Narvik. Stavanger was the air base from which the Luftwaffe mounted most of its attacks against the Home Fleet, so it was a prime target for attacks by Bomber Command. It was attacked at dusk on 11 April, by Wellingtons escorted by Coastal Command Blenheims who strafed the airfield before the bombing attacks by the Wellingtons, whose crews claimed to have started fires. One Wellington was lost in the attack.

The Whitley squadrons had been brought to immediate readiness on 9 April and were bombed up and ready to go, but they weren't sent until the night of the 11th. A force of twenty-three aircraft was sent to search for and bomb enemy shipping in the Skaggerack.

The weather wasn't good but there was some slight success. One aircraft attacked and destroyed a ship carrying ammunition while two more carried out attacks against ships but were unable to verify results because of the adverse weather.

Our crew took off at 18.45 hrs and set course. As we proceeded across the North Sea the weather conditions deteriorated and by the time we reached the Skaggerack we were flying in and out of snowstorms. I was incarcerated in the tail-turret where I was freezing. We carried out a 'Creeping Line Ahead' (CLA) search and despite the adverse conditions spotted an enemy ship. We attacked but were unfortunately prevented from assessing the result because it was snowing at the time – we hoped we'd been lucky.

We continued on our northerly course up the Oslo fjord and the frequency of the snowstorms increased. Ice formed on the wings and chunks flew off the propellers hitting the fuselage with alarming and resounding thuds. Snow swirled into my tail-turret and I had to keep moving the breech-block of my VGO back and forth to prevent it freezing up – I recall thinking there must be easier ways of earning a bonus of one shilling and sixpence a day!

When we were in the vicinity of Oslo we received the unwelcome attentions of the German flak-ships in the area. Some of the fire was fairly accurate and some of the shell-bursts were uncomfortably close to the tail. I was very glad when the skipper decided we'd done enough and set course for home. We landed at 03.30 hrs having been in the air for nine uncomfortable and frustrating hours. However we consoled ourselves that we were now dropping bombs instead of paper and who knows, we may have hit the ship we attacked. Before we left dispersal we discovered we'd sustained some slight flak damage. None of us had been hit but it was a reminder to be thankful for small mercies, especially when we heard the following day that one of our sister squadron's aircraft had failed to return.

On 12 April Wellingtons of No. 3 Group and Hampdens of No. 5 Group attempted to locate and attack units of the German Fleet which were reported to be heading south across the entrance to the Skaggerak. They were again unsuccessful because of the adverse weather conditions and also suffered the loss of eight of their number who were shot down by enemy fighters. It was another timely reminder that unescorted bombers were on a hiding to nothing from attacking fighters. However the lesson was partially learnt – from then on the Hampdens were restricted to night operations.

The raids against enemy-held airfields continued throughout the month of April, Blenheims attacking Stavanger in daylight, while the Whitleys attacked the other airfields by night, but all the raids were hampered by the continuing bad weather.

Our next sortie was against the airfield at Kjeller (Oslo) on the night of the 18/19th. We took off at 20.15 hours and as we proceeded over the North Sea the weather got progressively worse and when we reached the Oslo fjord it was atrocious. The whole area was obscured by snowstorms and although we descended to 500 feet we were unable to locate Kjeller airfield. We searched as long as our fuel stocks allowed but in the end, frozen and frustrated, we had to give it up – a thousand miles flog for nothing! Still we were luckier than some – one Whitley crew sent to attack shipping in the Trondheim fjord was forced to ditch in the icy sea; one crew member unfortunately drowned but the other four were miraculously rescued by a British destroyer.

Fornebu (Oslo) airfield was our target on the night of the 23rd/24th and again it was a case of making the best of a bad job. We again had to fly through snowstorms in the Oslo fjord which prevented us from locating the prime target, but during a rare clear period we managed to find and bomb the alternative, the airfield at Christiansund, however it didn't stay clear long enough for us to assess the result. A consolation was that the opposition was only slight. On our way home the weather at base deteriorated and we were diverted to Kinloss, where we landed after being airborne for ten long freezing hours, having not achieved much.

Our crew's next raid was on the night of 1/2 May and the target was Stavanger. The weather forecast was good for a change and surprise, surprise, it was correct! I think the 'Seaweed and Corn merchants' (Met men) threw a party to celebrate! Although we were the second aircraft off we were first to attack the target. As we approached Stavanger we could see it when we were still well out over the sea. The skipper throttled back the engines and we glided in and dropped our bombs on the airfield buildings from 2,000 feet. It was a complete surprise attack and as soon as the bomb-aimer called 'bombs gone', the skipper slammed open the throttles and we roared across the airfield as the bombs exploded. I had a grandstand view from the tail. The searchlights came on and attempted to illuminate us and the flak hosed after us. I retaliated strafing them with my VGO until all the rounds in the pan were exhausted. Fires started burning among the buildings as we escaped out to sea. We set course for home, highly elated having, in our estimation, done something 'destructive' for a change. When we got back to base we reckoned we'd earned our bacon and eggs. However the crews who had followed up our attack were highly uncomplimentary having had to cope with the hornets nest they accused us of stirring up.

During the campaign while the RAF carried out attacks against airfields and shipping, the Army, assisted by the Royal Navy, attempted to launch a counter-attack by land and sea. The Expeditionary Force had been assembling when it became clear that the Germans intended to invade Norway, but unfortunately they struck first.

On 9 April, a British brigade and three battalions of French troops were landed at Namsos in northern Norway. A second British brigade was landed at Aandalsnes with the object of taking possession of the port of Trondheim and the nearby airfield at Vaernes to prevent the Germans moving northwards.

Unfortunately, the Germans having first captured all the southern airfields had built up a force of fighters and bombers we in the RAF couldn't match. Our meagre fighter force (two squadrons), which had to operate from a frozen lake, was heavily outnumbered and wiped out within days although they fought most courageously. RAF Bomber Command did what it could but it was hampered by the awful weather and the added disadvantage of having to fly round trips of approximately 1,200 miles over open sea. Any hope of direct support for the ground forces was out of the question.

Our ground forces, who were completely out-gunned by German artillery, tanks and aircraft, had to withdraw. Fighting a gallant rearguard action they were evacuated by the Royal Navy on 30 April and 1 May while under heavy and continual air attack. There were still some Allied troops fighting further north in the Narvik area and they held out until 7 June when they were finally evacuated. So ended the 'Norwegian Nightmare', which cost us ships, aircraft, equipment and most important of all, gallant soldiers, sailors and airmen we could ill-afford to lose.

Four

Blitzkrieg

After the fall of Norway and Denmark the military situation changed dramatically and on 10 May, Hitlers's forces broke through the Allied defences of the west to invade Holland, Belgium and Luxemburg. This was to be closely followed by the breakthrough into France. The invasion commenced in the early hours of the 10th with an airborne assault on the Hague and Rotterdam. Meanwhile the Luftwaffe carried out mass raids on the Allied airfields and communications in Holland, Belgium and France. RAF and French Air Force fighters managed to get airborne in time to break up some of the enemy formations. They inflicted heavy losses on the enemy while incurring light losses themselves. On the other hand, the Dutch and Belgian Air Forces suffered heavily.

The Fairey Battle squadrons of the AASF (Advanced Air Striking Force) at their French bases were brought to immediate readiness at 06.00 hrs, but because of the indecision by the French Air Force Commander, it was noon before they were able to get airborne and only when the AOC (Air Officer Commanding) RAF Forces in France, on his own initiative, sent them to support to the hard pressed Allied ground troops. Also, because of disagreement between the British War Cabinet and the French War Council over which way they should be used, neither the two Blenheim squadrons of the AASF based in France, nor the UK-based light and heavy bombers were used in the early stages of the battle. It was only when the RAF Commander in France urgently requested them that the UK-based heavy bombers were used. On the night of 10 May thirty-six Wellingtons attacked Waalhaven airfield, while nine Whitleys bombed communications in southern Holland. The next night, thirty-six bombers comprising Whitleys and Hampdens attacked road and rail communications around Munchen Gladbach, the ban on attacking German land targets having been rescinded (a decision which was popularly received by the aircrew involved).

Our Squadron (10) had now converted and was equipped with the Whitley Mk V which among its modifications included a four-gun power operated tail turret, a welcome change for the tail-gunners from the open one-gun manually operated turret of the Mk IV. We were now protected from the elements and had four times the fire power.

On the night of 12/13 May our squadron took part in a raid on road and rail communications at Munchen Gladbach and my morale was boosted when I tested my new guns over the North Sea. As we crossed the coast near Amsterdam we could see the gunfire of the ground battle which was raging in the area. We had little opposition from the German defences until we reached the Munchen Gladbach target area when we were assailed by both searchlights and flak. As we glided in on our bomb-run from 9,000 feet,

I couldn't resist having a go with my new guns – I doubt whether I hit anything, but it took my mind off the flak which seemed to be getting uncomfortably close. After carrying out our attack we set course for home but I had scarcely recovered from the excitement of the bomb-run when I spotted a Me110 coming up on our port side above us. The adrenalin flow went into overdrive as I lined up the 110 in my reflector sight and gave a running commentary over the intercom. On instructions from the skipper I held my fire and the fighter continued on its way without seeing us – big sighs of relief all round. There were no more excitements and we returned to base without further incident.

From then on, things hotted up. On 15/16 May we were sent to bomb road and rail communications at Dinant in Belgium and it turned out to be a bit of a hairy one. The opposition wasn't too intense but after we'd bombed it was discovered that a 250lb bomb had 'hung up' in the bomb-bay and despite all our efforts to get rid of it we were unable to do so. We had a nail biting flight back to base and I think we all kept our fingers crossed during landing when it might have jolted off. Thankfully it didn't and the armourers were able to remove and defuse it – three cheers for the armourers!

Our next trip turned out to be a real 'shaky do'. The target was an oil storage depot at Bremen and because of the tank battle raging in France it was a vital objective. Our CO stressed its importance at briefing, reminding us that the destruction of the oil depot could adversely affect the invading German Panzers and mechanised forces in the Low Countries. Things didn't start very well. One of our aircraft crashed on take-off but fortunately the bombs didn't go up and there were no casualties. We were sitting in our aircraft waiting to taxi and saw it happen – not a great morale booster, but we got off safely and set course. When we reached the German coast we carefully avoided the defences at Wilhelmshaven and Bremerhaven and followed the River Weser to Bremen. As we got near the target the 'bods' up front reported that there was considerable flak and searchlight activity and fires were burning in the area, indicating the leading aircraft had done a good job – but in doing so they had stirred things up!

As the result of the CO's pep talk at briefing, the skipper decided we would carry out our attack gliding in from 4,000 feet. When we were on our bomb-run searchlights illuminated us and the flak batteries gave us their undivided attention. The tracers and incendiaries hosed up and were all around us as we made our bomb-run. As soon as the bomb-aimer called 'bombs gone', I belted away at the defences with my four Brownings while the skipper threw the aircraft all over the sky to get us out of the flak and searchlights. Eventually his violent evasive manoeuvres paid off and we escaped into the comforting darkness and set course for home. However we hadn't got off scot free. Luckily none us had been hit, but the aircraft was flying very sluggishly and it was discovered that it had been severely damaged. All the fabric had been shot away from the top of the port wing. We got home on the other wing (and a prayer) thankful for the robust construction of the Whitley and the skill and strength of our two pilots (newly promoted F/Lt Bickford and F/O Henry). We had learned before we took off that the skipper, F/Lt Bickford had been awarded the DFC. When he got us back safely from Bremen in the early hours, the rest of the crew all agreed he'd earned his gong. Shortly afterwards he left our crew, was promoted to S/Ldr and took over as Flight Commander 'B' Flight. F/O Henry was promoted to aircraft captain and took over the crew with F/O Wakefield taking his place as 2nd pilot/bomb-aimer.

He made his debut as captain on the night of the 21st/22nd when we were detailed to bomb road and rail communications at Julich near Cologne. The weather was fairly good so we were able to identify our target without much trouble and make our attack from 6,000 feet. There was considerable searchlight and flak opposition but thankfully it wasn't as severe as that we had encountered over Bremen. Before we left the target area I was able to give the defences their 'ration' of .303 from my tail guns. When we got back we found that we'd sustained some flak damage in the region of the tail – this operational flying was getting to be a bit dicey!

Because of the critical stage of the land battle, we were on again that night, being detailed to attack road and rail communications at Givet on the Franco/Belgian border. Givet was an important junction through which the Germans were supporting their breakthrough. It was heavily defended with batteries of mobile 20mm and 37mm flak guns and they made it hot for us as we bombed, but luckily we got through safely. On the way back we received a W/T message to divert to Kidlington near Oxford because of deteriorating weather at base. We landed there safely despite the hazards of having to dodge numerous Tiger Moths carrying out night circuits and bumps. The higher-ranking members of the crew were accommodated in their respective messes while Fletch and myself were ensconced in the airmen's transit billet. Having done two raids on the trot we needed no rocking! In the afternoon the weather cleared up and we returned to base. After our two consecutive 'Ops' we were given the night off. For some it was a chance to relax, for others an opportunity to whoop it up in the nearby town.

We were back on the job the following night, 24/25th, and our targets were road and rail communications at Binche in Belgium. The weather was fairly good and after we'd crossed the coast, Arthur Knapper our observer (navigator) took us to the town of Charleroi and followed the road to Binche. From there the bomb-aimer was able to map-read us to the target. He was aided by the defence activity obviously stirred up by the crews proceeding us. As we made our run over the target we were obviously the only aircraft there at the time because the defences gave us their undivided attention. However we pressed on and bombed, then as soon as we could we high tailed it out of the area, but as we were congratulating ourselves we'd got away with it once again the bomb-aimer reported that a 250lb bomb had been left hung up on the rack. We tried to get rid of it but it stuck like ★★★★ to a blanket, so we had a repeat nail-biting return flight, again we were lucky to land safely without the rogue bomb dropping off. Again the brave armourers removed and defused it. In such circumstances the aircraft is evacuated with incredible speed once it lands! It was another case of two on the trot because we were on again that night, the 26/27th. This time the target was an oil plant at Rheisholz in the Ruhr. It turned out to be a fairly uneventful sortie, but it could have been otherwise.

The skipper decided that as we'd been hit on the last trip when we were fairly low, this time we would make our attack from 12,000 feet where we hoped we'd be out of range of the light flak. It worked out just as he'd hoped and we were able to bomb and get through the target safely, but just when we were relaxing and settling down on our way home, a Me110 joined us on a parallel course. I lined him up in my sight and watched him like a hawk. He stayed on the same course for about three minutes then turned away – the relief was audible!

Since the beginning of the bombing war (10 April – the invasion of Norway) to the end of May, 4 Group had suffered casualties. Twelve aircraft had failed to return through enemy action, five had crash-landed on return from sorties, two crews had baled out on return, one had ditched, two had crashed on take-off and there had been eighteen instances of flak damage. We were learning the hard way. Despite our losses we were thankful we weren't flying the Fairey Battles or Blenheims of the AASF in France who were suffering crippling losses. That wasn't the only grim news, the land battle was going very badly and coming to its tragic conclusion. On 26th May, Operation Dynamo, the evacuation of our surviving troops from Dunkirk was initiated.

The only crumb of comfort we received at that time was the decision of the Air Ministry, with effect from 27 May, that all operational WOp/AGs and AGs – who up to now had been flying in their 'tradesman' rank of aircraftsmen – would be promoted to the rank of Sergeant with a new rate of pay instead of trade pay plus one and sixpence a day flying pay. Also, in future Sergeant rank would be awarded on successful completion of training. While we survivors welcomed this long overdue decision, it was too late for the 200 WOp/AGs and AGs who had been killed in action since 3 September 1939.

By 4 June, the evacuation of our troops from Dunkirk was complete but what was left of our Fairey Battle oppos of the AASF fought on as the German advance continued. In the meantime aircraft of Bomber Command, including our Whitley Group, continued attacks against enemy troops and transport in France and the Low countries and oil targets in Germany.

To add to our misfortunes Italy declared war on France and Britain on 10 June and in retaliation the Whitley Group carried out the first raid on Italy with a force of thirty-six aircraft. Using the civil airfields in the Channel Islands, they attacked the Fiat Works on the night of the 11/12th. Our crew was with the force which pre-positioned at Guernsey during the afternoon of the 11th. For most of the force it turned out to be a shaky and frustrating experience, first having to take-off from a 800 yards runway with full bomb and petrol load, then having to climb over the Alps in the most horrible weather conditions. Only twelve Whitleys managed to get through the storm and bomb the target. Two failed to get airborne, twenty aborted because they iced-up and couldn't climb over the Alps. One bombed an alternative target and one failed to return. We were one of the number that aborted after icing-up and being struck by lightning. We did an about turn and scrambled back to land safely after six uncomfortable and frustrating hours. The only consolation was that the twelve crews (which included our CO) who managed to get through and bomb, claimed that they had really clobbered the target.

The Whitley Group resumed bombing road and rail communications in France and the marshalling-yards in Germany but on the night of 14/15 June, they gave us another task, dropping mines in the River Rhine to destroy oil barges. The mines which were known as 'W' bombs, a new secret weapon invented by scientists and inventors gathered together by the Government at the beginning of the war to explore all possible avenues to carry the war to the enemy

As a schoolboy I used to buy the weekly magazines in circulation at the time, such as *The Wizard*, *The Rover* and *The Magnet*. Sometimes they included stories concerning eccentric inventors and chemistry professors, whose experiments usually resulted in them staggering tattered and smoke-blackened from their laboratories as their efforts once again ended in disaster. At the time I believed that these professors were the figment of the author's imagination – I was wrong! They were alive and kicking and dreaming up weapons for use by unsuspecting bomber crews!

This 'W' Bomb was the first of them. It was to be dropped in Germany's canals and rivers to destroy barges and bridges – a worthwhile project, but the bombs couldn't be dropped from heights above 1,000 feet or at speeds above 250mph. The speed restriction was no problem – the Whitley would be pushed to achieve 250mph in a screaming dive, never mind straight and level on a bomb-run. It was the height limit that bothered us – they wanted us to stooge around Hunland in the dark at 1,000 feet, surely they must be joking – they weren't!

On the night of 14/15 June twelve Whitley crews were lumbered with their dirty work. It turned out to be a miserable failure, only two of the crews being able to drop their bombs as briefed. Our crew was involved in the next attempt on the night of 16/17 June as eleven aircraft were detailed. Again it was a disaster, only four crews claiming to have dropped their bombs as specified. We were briefed to drop our bombs in the Rhine south of Bingen, near Mannheim. The weather was far from good, cloud base 2,000 feet with visibility underneath restricted by rain and industrial haze. In these conditions we had difficulty in locating the Rhine, never mind the precise dropping area and it nearly ended in disaster. Flying down the Rhine at 2,000 feet we blundered into the defences protecting Mannheim and it's a miracle they didn't blast us out of the sky, but we managed to escape. Foolishly we had another go but when the defences again nearly knocked seven bells out of us, the skipper wisely decided this was no game for stalwart young airmen to be playing so we left the area smartly and set course for home, which we reached safely, still cursing the boffins!

There was a tragic sequel to the 'W' Bomb saga. On the morning of 22 June, an explosion occurred in our bomb-dump resulting in the deaths of two of our armourers – they were defusing 'W' Bombs at the time. As a result the powers that be abandoned the project and it was agreed, especially by the aircrew, that it wasn't before time.

On 22 June, the French Government signed an Armistice, having sued for peace on 16 June. The remnants of the AASF squadrons flew back to the UK, while same French squadrons flew to Africa opting to fly with the British in the Middle East. The blitzkrieg mounted by the Germans had triumphed and now Great Britain stood alone. The following months were to be vital for the survival of freedom.

Flak damage Bremen, 17 May 1940.

No. 10 Whitley Squadron aircrew, RAF Dishforth, April 1940.

Bomb-aimers' position, Whitley Mark V.

Two Mark V Whitleys of No. 10 Squadron.

4-gun Frazer-Nash Turret.

Bombs for Berlin, September 1940.

Five
Battle for Britain

On 3 July, the Luftwaffe, operating from its newly captured bases in France began a series of raids against our English Channel ports and our shipping in the English Channel. This, it was surmised, was a portent of invasion and as part of our anti-invasion strategy, RAF bomber squadrons were instructed to have aircraft and crews on standby.

In the meantime our bombing attacks continued against targets which included docks, ports, battleships in harbour, marshalling-yards, aircraft parks and oil installations. On 24 July however, the Air Staff directed that from now on the heavy bomber force was to concentrate on attacks against fifteen selected strategic targets in Germany; five aircraft storage depots, five airframe assembly factories and five oil installations. Attacks on communications were also to continue but only on a limited scale. Until the Allied Invasion of Europe, Bomber Command would be the only means of carrying the fight to Germany proper.

Also during July the Air Staff introduced a system of 'screening' bomber aircrew after they had carried out a certain number of raids. Thirty was selected as the number of operations which would constitute a tour. These screened aircrew were then posted to instruct at the various Operational Training Units which had been established. The purpose of these being to train new crews and to give the operational aircrew a rest while they imparted the knowledge gained on Ops to the new crews. Fletch our 1st WOp/AG and 'Nipper' our Observer were posted under the new arrangements. However, it's tragic to relate that Fletch having survived his tour was killed two months later on a training flight at the OTU. Unfortunately, this was to happen time and again throughout the war. Also at this time F/O Wakefield, our 2nd pilot/bomb-aimer was posted and replaced by F/O Landale. When Fletch left, I took over as 1st WOp/AG, my replacement as tail-gunner/2nd WOp, being an oppo George Dove who was waiting to qualify as a first operator. Nipper was replaced by 'G.B.' Shaw, an observer who had a few more trips to do to finish his tour.

Our new crew made its debut on the night of 24 July, our target being the port of Hamburg, where the German battleship *Bismark* and the liners *Bremen* and *Europa* were supposed to be berthed. Unfortunately the weather was atrocious and the port obscured by cloud from ground level upwards. On ETA it was obvious we were in the target area from the flak bursting around us, but we were unable to bomb and, observing instructions to avoid indiscriminate bombing, the bombs were brought back. The trip wasn't all disaster, I was commended in the Squadron Operations Record book, for having obtained a number of Loop (radio) fixes which enabled the aircraft to be brought back with remarkable navigational accuracy. Although the bad weather persisted operations continued to the end of the month against marshalling-yards and aircraft factories.

Our skipper, F/O Henry (Enery) with whom I'd flown since the beginning of the war, was, like our old skipper, awarded the DFC. I suppose the two awards could be looked upon as a reflection of the courage, efficiency and devotion to duty of the crew as a whole! However, it is also worth taking note that during the first year of the war all the awards to our squadron were to pilots only!

At the beginning of August the Luftwaffe attacks over the Channel and the south of England increased and on 12 August, their efforts to knock out Fighter Command began in earnest. However, they found out they had bitten off more than they could chew, as our fighter boys continued to shoot them down.

In the meantime we in Bomber Command continued our attacks against strategic targets. On the night of 2/3 August, our crew, with others, attacked an oil refinery at Salzbergen and on the 4/5th a Dornier aircraft factory at Wismar. Bad weather interfered and no further ops were carried out until the 9/10th when we attacked industrial targets at Ludwigshaven, followed by an attack against Frankfurt-am-Main.

Oil was at the top of the target list on the night of the 11/12th, when we attacked Gelsenkirchen and Frankfurt. It was during this raid that the dreaded boffins struck again with another supposed secret weapon. Their fiendish plan this time was for us to drop incendiary 'leaves' codenamed 'Razzle' on the stocks of arms and warlike stores supposedly stashed in the Black Forest.

The incendiary device was a pill of phosphorous covered by gauze inserted between two squares of celluloid. They were carried in sealed cans of water (to prevent them from drying out and igniting spontaneously) and stacked in racks in the aircraft fuselage. The boffins had it all worked out! After bombing our primary target (if we were still around), we were then to fly over the Black Forest and scatter the Razzle on the stocks of arms etc. The 'leaves' would dry out, spontaneous combustion would take place and set fire to the stores. That was the plan.

Our crew's primary target was Gelsenkirchen, where the German defences did their utmost to knock us out of the sky, but we bombed successfully and then made our way to the Black Forest to drop the Razzle. On arrival at the dropping zone I made my way to the fuselage – as usual the 1st WOp was lumbered with this additional task. I diligently poured the Razzle down the flare-chute as per instructions then after I'd finished checked that there were no 'leaves' stuck in the chute. If there had been, the Boffin's instructions were: 'If you can't get rid of them out of the aircraft, don't let them dry out, keep spraying them with water from the garden-syringe provided!' Bloody comedians!

I returned to my wireless position completely unaware that some of the dreaded things on leaving the chute had been caught in the slipstream and had lodged in the tail-plane elevator hinges, on the tail-plane itself and even on the tail-wheel. On our return flight they began to dry out!

We got back to base safely and taxied back to dispersal, relieved and relaxing with the thought that we'd made it again, when our tail-gunner George Dove reported that the fabric on the elevators was burning merrily. Fortunately our ground-crew were able to extinguish the flames before any serious damage was done. Practically all the aircraft

Razzling that night suffered the same fate. Later it was reported that the only damage Razzle inflicted on the Germans was when some of them finding the 'leaves' put them in their pockets as souvenirs and when they dried out they apparently got more than their fingers burnt!

Because of bad weather persisting over Germany attacks were switched to targets in Italy. From advanced bases in the south of England we were one of the crews involved, but again we didn't make it – as we were climbing to get over the Alps we lost an engine and had to return. Another flog for nothing, but I suppose we were lucky to make it home on our one good engine.

As the tempo of the German efforts to knock out the RAF increased, they mounted a mass attack against the Whitley bases in the north of England on 15 August. They must have been under the mistaken impression that all our fighters were heavily committed in the south. This, of course, was not so and our northern-based fighters inflicted heavy losses, but some of the attackers got through and one of our Whitley bases, (Driffield) was heavily hit, severe damage being inflicted on parked aircraft and installations. Fortunately casualties were relatively light.

On the night of 16/17 August, we were back attacking targets in Germany, our target being the Zeiss optical works at Jena, where we encountered only slight opposition enabling us to carry out four separate bomb-runs at 5,000 feet – an easy trip for a change.

It was a different story on the night of 18/19 August, when we attempted to bomb an aluminium factory at Rheinfellen. The weather was bad when we took off and it got progressively worse as we flew across Germany. We were practically tossed from one cu-nim to another and at our estimated time of arrival over the target we were unable to locate it. It wasn't our night. We set course for our alternative, but we were again unsuccessful and to make things worse we were struck by lightning which burnt off the W/T trailing aerial. Our misfortune continued when the generator supplying H/T power to my transmitter packed in. However, GBS our observer was on the ball with his Dead Reckoning and got us back to base after nine frustrating hours.

Because of the prevailing bad weather we were able to have a short respite, but we were back on the job on the night of 24/25 August when we were detailed to attack a target at Milan. This would be mine and Enery's third attempt to get to Italy and according to him we were going to get there even if we had to get out and push! However, this time we were lucky, everything worked like clockwork, the weather was good, we were able to get over the Alps without difficulty, pinpoint the target and because the opposition was only moderate, we were able to make two bombing-runs. The bomb-aimer, together with our tail-gunner for that trip (P/O Neal) claimed we had really clobbered the target and to make it a good night all round we had an uneventful return flight and got safely back to base after being airborne for nearly nine hours.

That was our skipper's (Enery's) last trip with us and he left us to join the first Halifax squadron (35), but sadly he was killed on 11 January 1941, while carrying out an air test. We had flown together since the beginning of the war and the strict discipline and class gulf which existed in the peacetime Air Force between officers and other ranks, had diminished as time passed. I like to think that before he left the crew, because we'd endured some hairy do's together, we'd established some mutual respect without adversely affecting crew discipline.

By this time I'd participated in thirty-four raids and as the majority of my regular aircrew oppos who I had been with since the beginning of the war had now departed in one way or another. I was getting the impression that in my case the screening system wasn't working. After the Milan trip I went off to have some leave and it was a welcome relief not to have to endure the throb of Merlins, the cacophony of Morse Code and static interference pounding in my head – if only for a few days. My leave, as always, passed too quickly and I returned to the squadron to find that our crew had been re-organised. Our second pilot (F/O Landale) had been promoted to captain, 'GBS' our observer had been screened and replaced by P/O Dickenson and we had a new second pilot, F/O Boxwell. George Dove, tail-gunner, and myself were the only two old hands in the crew, the others being very inexperienced.

By this time, the beginning of September, the battle for Britain was reaching a crucial climax. Our fighter boys had denied the Germans the air superiority necessary to support an invasion. Also, from early September to the end of the month, Bomber Command played a decisive part, carrying out continuous day and night attacks against the German invasion fleets massing in the Channel ports of Ostend, Antwerp, Calais, Dunkirk and Boulogne. The losses and damage caused to these fleets during our bombing attacks were a significant factor in the postponement and eventual cancellation of Hitler's Invasion, Operation Sea Lion. It is worth remembering that our bombing raids cost us a high price and that during the battle for Britain, Bomber Command casualties exceeded those of Fighter Command. While in no way denigrating the magnificent achievement and sacrifice by our Fighter Boys, it is unfortunate that the bomber crews were not afforded the same well-deserved recognition.

Our new skipper and crew was checked out by F/O 'Pinpoint' Prior (one of the squadron's senior pilots) on the raids to the Channel Port of Ostend on 8/9 September, but we were frustrated once again by the adverse weather. We made up for it on the night of 11/12th when we attacked Bremen. Ever since that very shaky do in May with my original crew, I'd had a very healthy respect for the Bremen defences, which were now even more formidable, but we managed to bomb the target successfully and stoke up the fires started by the early attackers. Our tail-gunner reported he could still see the fires when we were some fifty miles into our return flight. Our crew was given the OK by Pinpoint.

On the night of the 14/15th the weather improved over the Channel Ports and we were able to attack the barges and shipping at Antwerp. I flew as tail-gunner for this trip giving George Dove the opportunity of getting some key-bashing (wireless operating) practice as he was about to leave us and take over as 1st WOp/AG with another crew. We were able to attack the target successfully despite severe opposition and after our bomb-run I was able to report a massive explosion in the target area. On our way home I saw a Me110 above us and focused him in my reflector sight, but thankfully he proceeded on his way without seeing us.

We had an abortive trip to Hamburg on the night of the 17/18th and had to return because of a tail-turret malfunction, but we made up for it two nights later when we successfully attacked the marshalling-yards at Hamm. This was always a well-defended target and they gave us a pasting, especially during our bomb-run. As usual I was down by the flare-chute dropping parachute flares to illuminate the target as well as dropping my personal contribution of surplus loose incendiaries. These were supposed to be used for drift-finding but if there were any spare I always got rid of them over the target – why not! When we went through the worst of the flak I heard the tinkling sounds as some of the shrapnel hit us. We weren't hit seriously and we got away smartly after the bombs had gone. I crawled through the tunnel to the cockpit and returned to my wireless position. As I was levering myself into my seat I rested my hand on my open W/T Logbook. When I took it away the pages were covered in blood which was seeping from my leather gauntlet. I eased off my glove and the blood-stained silk inner to find a sliver of metal protruding from the fleshy part of my hand. I removed the splinter carefully and bound my wound with my handkerchief. Our new observer Tubby who was only on his fourth trip, blanched when he saw the gore, but I reassured him that I wasn't mortally wounded. I felt little discomfort and as the damage was to my left hand it didn't affect my operating the W/T. We got back to base safely where I had to suffer a certain amount of leg-pulling about my wound.

While the attacks against the Invasion Ports continued, raids were also mounted against strategic targets and on 21/22 September we were involved in carrying out an attack against an aluminium factory at Lauta, deep in the heart of Germany. It was a virgin target and as it hadn't been attacked previously we were under the impression it might be an easy touch. How wrong can you be! By the time we got there the early birds had really stirred things up and the natives were very hostile. Despite this we managed to make two bomb-runs and as we left the target our new tail-gunner, Sgt Slim Somerville reported that fires were burning. On our way home the electrical storms we'd encountered on our way to the target had increased and adversely affected the capacity to obtain W/T bearings and fixes. Between us though, our new observer and myself managed to cope navigationally – even though we were struck by lightning which again burnt off the trailing aerial. We scrambled back after being airborne for ten and a half hours and as we turned off the flare-path after landing, one of our engines cut out – we'd run out of gravy!

We had another eventful trip on the 24/25th. Our primary target was a power station at Finkenheerd, sixty miles east of Berlin near Frankfurt-on-Oder. Again the weather was grim and we flew in and out of cloud all the way there and when we reached the target area we were still in it. We stooged around looking for a break, but we were unable to find one so we decided to go for our alternative target, Templhof airfield, Berlin.

On the way the cloud started to break but when we got to Berlin we were unable to pinpoint the airfield. However, through a break we spotted the main railway station, so we decided to have a go at that. At this time we must have been the only aircraft over Berlin so we had the defences all to ourselves and didn't they let us know it! As we commenced our bomb-run the bomb-aimer complained the cloud was obscuring the target and he might have to take us around for a second run! He was advised to have another think and if he couldn't see railway lines, tram lines would do as by this time the flak was coming up thick and fast. His eyesight improved immediately, he took us in over the target and dropped the bombs! As soon as he called, 'bombs gone', we were away like 'Flynn' back into the clouds where we deluded ourselves we could avoid the flak. We were lucky, we got away without a scratch and were able to continue unhindered on our way across Germany and the North Sea to our planned diversion airfield. When we landed there we had been in the air for ten hours and forty minutes, my forty-first and longest operational trip. I was coming to the conclusion that the screening bods had forgotten me and were being most unfair, particularly to nineteen-year-olds and especially yours truly!

We were off again on the 27/28th to bomb the German submarine installations at the French port of Lorient. This made a change from spending hours over Germany dodging the defences on our way to the target. On this trip we were able to stooge down to the south coast of England, cross the Channel and then the north-west corner of Occupied France. From there we were able to get a good pinpoint, map-read our way to the target and make our bomb-run. The opposition was, I am pleased to say, light compared with that we'd encountered over some of our previous targets. After our attack the bomb-aimer claimed our bombs had fallen on the target and as we left the area the tail-gunner reported that fires were burning. We had an uneventful return flight and I suppose this trip could be classed as an easy one – for a change!

The morning and night of 30 September were to be memorable for me. During the morning the Group Signals Officer paid a visit to our W/T Section ostensibly to have a morale-boosting chat to the WOp/AGs. In the course of his conversation he asked us in turn how many raids we'd done. When he learned how many I'd done he did a double-take and told me something I'd been trying to get across for weeks – that I had passed my shelf-life and should have been screened before now. His reaction was to contact our CO and inform him that he proposed to get in touch with Group HQ immediately to have me screened and posted to instruct at an OTU without delay. I accepted his decision without demur, knowing full well that you can push your luck just so far. With the usual youthful arrogance and bravado I suppose I kidded myself I was fire-proof and that it was always the other blokes who would get the chop, but in the dark recesses of my mind I knew full well that I was only concealing the fear that my time might be running out. I was very relieved that I was going to be screened at long last.

Later that day however, my elation and relief was shattered when I was informed that I was on ops again that night, and my morale lowered even more at briefing when I discovered that our target was the Reich Chancellery in Berlin. Also I would be flying with a 'scratch' crew. My skipper F/O Landale having been involved in an accident was replaced by F/Lt Tomlinson and F/Lt Clarke, the Group Gunnery Leader would be flying as our tail-gunner, instead of Slim Somerville. To record I wasn't bothered would be a downright lie – I suppose I was as scared as I've ever been, but somebody must have been watching out for me because the trip to the target wasn't too bad, apart from a jolt to my morale when we were passing south of Wilhelmshaven and saw the flak batteries knocking hell out of some poor sods. However we pressed on and avoided the defences en route, but when we got to Berlin we had to run the gauntlet of those formidable defences. During the bomb-run I was back in the fuselage dropping flares and although I couldn't see much of the flak, I could feel its effects and I'll always remember the tone of urgency in F/Lt Clarke's voice as he reported the proximity of the shell bursts to his turret!

Thankfully we were able to bomb and get away unscathed, but the return flight was, for me, interminable. I can't describe my feeling of relief when I saw the airfield beacon winking its friendly code as we were able to join the circuit and land – hurrah! My extended tour was over. A few days later I was posted to No. 19 OTU RAF Kinloss for my 'rest'.

Six

An Uneasy Rest

I was given a few days leave before taking up my instructional post at the Whitley OTU at RAF Kinloss on the Moray Firth. On arrival I was pleased to renew acquaintance with other Whitley aircrew who had survived their tour of operations and who were now on rest as instructors. During our mini-reunion in the Sergeants' Mess on my first evening, they gave me the gen on the training set-up. Apparently the OTU comprised two flights, an Anson flight used primarily for navigation training and a Whitley flight for crew operational training.

The following morning I reported to the OTU HQ where I was interviewed by the Officer Commanding, W/Cdr L.S. Snaith AFC. As an F/O he had been a member of the pre-war RAF High Speed Flight Team at RAF Calshot, which broke the World Speed Flying Record at the then fantastic speed of 404 mph and won the Schneider trophy outright for Great Britain in 1931.

After reviewing my operational record he informed me I would be joining the Whitley Flight and welcomed me to the unit, adding that although this was supposed to be a rest period, I might not get much rest. This was because of the necessity to get as many new crews operationally trained as soon as possible and posted to the squadrons, where they were urgently needed to replace losses and tour-expired crews.

Before I left his office I took the opportunity to mention my ambition to remuster as pilot and asked when it might be possible to apply to do so. His reaction was to inform me instructional staff were required to complete a minimum of six months at the OTU and to put any ideas to the contrary on hold! However he did offer some hope by advising me that if I applied in six months time he would consider progressing my application.

So, I was absorbed into the Whitley Flight and crewed to fly with P/O T.G. 'Hamish' Mahaddie, an ex-77 Squadron pilot who had recently completed an eventful operational tour. He later made a name for himself when he went back to fly a second operational tour, this time on Stirlings, and he eventually ended up as a highly decorated member of Air Vice-Marshal D.T.C. Bennet's Pathfinder Group staff.

The training syllabus followed the system of dual instruction until the pupil crew reached a required solo standard, when they were sent on solo exercises to complete their training. However I was to discover that when they went on their solo flights they weren't quite 'on their own'. Apparently an order existed to the effect that on every flight a WOp/AG instructor must accompany them! I asked the other WOp/AG instructors the reason for this and was given the incomprehensible reply, 'in case problems arose'. While it was obvious the WOp/AG instructors had the flying and operational experience on the

Whitley, I couldn't understand how they were supposed to be capable of dealing with every emergency situation which might arise. My fellow instructors were of the same opinion as myself but being 'disciplined unquestioning' regulars, they were accepting this bizarre situation under duress. Later it is alleged one WOp/AG instructor who refused to fly in such circumstances was threatened with losing his sergeant rank and being relegated to Airman General Duty (dogsbody) status!

The sergeant in question, who had been awarded the Distinguished Flying Medal during his operational tour, protested against this draconian treatment and, with some assistance, got himself posted back on operations for a second tour. On his first trip he apparently performed an act of bravery which resulted in him being awarded the Conspicuous Gallantry Medal! From then on it was rumoured he insisted on being addressed as Sergeant *******, CGM DFM LMF!

There were, unfortunately, many instances throughout the war of so-called Lack of Moral Fibre episodes when aircrew senior NCQs were stripped of their rank. This punishment did not always apply to aircrew officers who refused to fly – except in the most severe circumstances. They were quietly posted from the unit to some backwater for the duration, but they retained their rank.

We were kept busy training the replacement crews because, as the Wingco had pointed out, it was a matter of urgency. During the period of June to the end of September 1940 (which encompassed the Battle of Britain) the Whitley Group had suffered the following casualties – 26 aircraft had failed to return from ops, there were 8 ditchings, 3 crashes on take-off, 22 crash-landings on return, 5 bale-outs and 32 instances of flak damage – resulting in over 50% fatalities plus injuries to the 480 aircrew involved.

The need to replace these losses as soon as possible may have influenced the amount of operational flying training the replacement crews received. Consequently some them ended up being sent to the squadrons with the minimum know-how needed to cope with the stress of flying on ops. Others didn't even make it to the squadrons, becoming casualties in crashes during training. A number of fatal crashes occurred during the first few weeks I was at the OTU and I came to the conclusion that I had maybe jumped out of the frying-pan only to end up in the fire! Especially when I heard that Johnny Fletcher, my ex-crewmate had been killed on a training flight from 10 OTU, RAF Abingdon, where he had been sent on rest.

One of the crashes which occurred involved an Anson of ours on a night cross-country exercise while flying over a remote part of Scotland, and the search parties didn't find it for six weeks. During the searches they discovered the wreckage of a First World War Sopwith Camel!

I soldiered on diligently instructing and in April 1941 I was promoted Flight Sergeant. By this time my six months rest period was officially over so I recommenced submitting my applications; first to remuster as pilot and when that brought no result, I applied to remuster as Wireless Operator Mechanic (a step-up in my basic trade).

By the beginning of June 1941, I'd received nothing to indicate that my applications were receiving attention, however I did hear on the grapevine that my first operational skipper (S/Ldr R. Bickford DFC) had gone back on operations with 76 Squadron to do a second tour on the new four-engined Halifax. I contacted him (via unofficial channels) and indicated that a fellow WOp/AG instructor, F/Sgt Chas Armstrong and myself, were now eligible to return to operations having completed our instructional tour and wouldn't mind doing another operational tour. The result was that we were both posted to join him on 11 July 1941 on the newly-formed Halifax squadron. This happened just before our CO issued a directive to the effect that all applications for posting had to be made through official channels – we'd made it just in time! However, before we left the OTU when we were interviewed by him, he thanked us for our work at the OTU, but hoped we weren't 'pushing our luck' going back on ops.

He was right, we realised we were pushing our luck, but being at the age when you kid yourself you're invulnerable, we decided we would rather take our chances on ops again rather than continue risking our necks at the OTU.

Seven
Pushing Our Luck

After completing the clearance procedure at the OTU, Chas Armstrong and myself left RAF Kinloss early on 11 July by train on our journey to RAF Middleton-St-George, near Darlington, to join 76 Squadron. Travelling on wartime trains was never a picnic, what with partially heated, blacked-out carriages and constant changes – our journey was no exception.

We arrived at Darlington railway station in the early hours of the 12th and telephoned the MT section at Middleton, requesting transport. After some considerable delay a three-tonner arrived and as we climbed aboard the driver informed us that our new squadron was operating that night so MT was at a premium. He dropped us off at the Sergeants' Mess where we off-loaded our kit and made our way to the kitchen to scrounge a cuppa from the duty cook to help us recover from our long and uncomfortable train journey. He obliged, and after consuming a welcome steaming hot mug of char our next task was to find a room where we could get our heads down. However, being compassionate characters we refrained from dragging the Duty Sergeant from his warm bed to fix us up with a room, instead we retired to the mess lounge where we curled up on settees for the rest of the night.

We rose early, made ourselves presentable and went to the dining room for breakfast. There were one or two early birds already there, toying with their soya-link bangers and yellow peril (dried egg), so we joined them and got into conversation during which we elicited information about the Station in general and our new squadron in particular.

After breakfast, following the directions we'd been given, we made our way to the hangar where the squadron offices were located. We reported to the Squadron Adjutant who welcomed us to the unit and gave us a quick run down on the squadron set-up and its personalities, before ushering us into the CO's office to make our number.

Our interview with W/Cdr T.G. Jarman DFC, OC 76 Squadron was brief. 'Let me see your logbooks, hmm, come for a second tour. Right, got your flying-kit with you? Good, we'll see about getting you crewed up, in the meantime get yourselves booked in and accommodated, then report to the W/T and Gunnery sections and get genned up on the Halifax. No doubt I'll see you later'. 'Yes Sir' – smart salaam and exeunt pronto!

Returning to the Adjutant's office I asked him if it would be possible to see S/Ldr Bickford, my old skipper. His reply was bad news. He told me that the S/Ldr was in hospital having been wounded two nights previously during a raid on Leuna when his aircraft was attacked by a Me110 night-fighter which had shot away most of his instrument panel and the windscreen. To get home he had the crew place the compass (which had been knocked from its mounting to the floor), on his lap, and to strap a torch to his harness. Despite his wound and having to endure the freezing cold slipstream through the damaged windscreen he got the aircraft back safely. The adjutant said that luckily his injury wasn't serious and as it turned out he was only in hospital for a few days before being sent on sick leave.

So I had to wait until he returned to duty before I was able to thank him for rescuing Chas and myself from the OTU. During our chat he told me that as he was now senior Flight Commander, he didn't fly with a regular crew, but no doubt we would fly together again in the future. Fate however, decreed otherwise.

Although he must have been feeling the effects of his injury, being a press on type, he led the squadron aircraft participating in a raid on Frankfurt on the night of the 30/31 August. On the outbound leg, to make sure he got there first, he used a bit of extra boost and consequently more fuel. After carrying out the bombing run he spent some time flying around the target area assessing the results of his and the follow-up attacks. The result was that he used more fuel than planned and when they got back over England, they were getting dangerously short. Unfortunately before they could divert to refuel, two engines cut out on one side. The early Halifax series unfortunately didn't have enough control to maintain direction or height with two engines failed on one side, so the S/Ldr gave the order to bale out. Five of the crew got out safely, but tragically he and the tail-gunner were killed. A sad end to a gallant flier and skipper who had always commanded the utmost respect.[1]

Chas Armstrong and I were settling in the squadron, getting genned up on the new W/T equipment (the Marconi T1154/R1155 which had replaced the pre-war T1083/R1082) and the Boulton Paul gun turrets with which the Halifax was equipped. It was while we were undergoing our conversion that the squadron was involved in a daylight raid on the German battle cruiser *Scharnhorst* at La Pallice, 200 miles south of Brest on 24 July 1941.

They were part of a Halifax force comprising fifteen aircraft (nine from 35 Squadron and six from our 76 Squadron). Being unescorted they received a hostile reception from enemy fighters as they approached the target and then as they made their attack they had to run the gauntlet through the flak.

Despite this most got through and the crews claimed hits on the target. However, the losses were high. Two Halifaxes were shot down before they reached the target and three went down over the target. Out of the six sent from our squadron one turned back because of engine trouble and three were shot down. Among the decorations awarded after the raid was a DSO to our CO W/Cdr Jarman, who had led the squadron.

The squadron was also involved in further daylight raids on the *Scharnhorst* and *Gneisnau* at Brest during December. On the 18th, a combined force of eighteen Halifaxes, eighteen Stirlings and eleven Manchesters (this time escorted by Spitfires fitted with long-range tanks) carried out an attack.

Although no serious damage was inflicted on the warships, the bomber force losses were comparatively light – four Stirlings, one Halifax and one Manchester. The next daylight raid on the warships was on 30 December, by sixteen Halifaxes again escorted by Spitfires. Unfortunately the results of the attack were disappointing. Three Halifaxes were shot down and most of the others sustained considerable flak damage.

In the meantime the squadron had continued its night raids against German land targets. On the night of 12/13 August, three aircraft were sent to bomb Berlin. One aircraft was shot down over the target, another was shot down near Bremen (this one was captained by Leonard Cheshire's brother Christopher – he and four of his crew managed to bale out and were taken prisoner). The third aircraft attacked successfully but unfortunately crashed on landing back at base, killing all the crew. This period, when these crippling losses were being inflicted on Bomber Command, was the Command's 'slough of despond' when the chances of completing a full tour of thirty raids was rated as only 40%.

Having been away from the operational scene for eight months, Chas and I had a lot to catch up with, so we spent some time in the Station Intelligence Section, absorbing the up-to-date information available concerning operational procedures and latest Intelligence reports on the German defences.

The IO (Intelligence Officer) F/Lt 'Skip' Seymour, a Reservist who had flown with the Royal Flying Corps during the First World War, informed us that Air Ministry was now encouraging aircrew to learn a personal code, so that in the event of being shot down and taken prisoner, they could pass back useful information in their subsequent letters home. Chas and myself were both keen to participate so we learnt the code and provided a specimen coded letter which Skip passed to Air Ministry for future reference – though we sincerely hoped the occasion wouldn't arise. Skip appreciated our enthusiasm and involved us in another experiment which was being carried out at the time, with regard to replacing the current flying boots i.e. black leather or suede knee-length boots, with a new type to facilitate evasion in the event of being shot down.

The new type flying boots were made of fleece-lined black leather, also knee-length, but instead of the usual strap and buckle, they had lace-up shoes sewn onto the uppers, the idea being that after a successful bale out and landing, the uppers could be detached leaving the wearer with a pair of shoes. A small pocket-knife was concealed in one of the boot legs to cut off the uppers.

Two pairs were sent to each operational Bomber Station for trial and as Chas and I happened to be there when they arrived and had the correct shoe size, they were issued to us. I found that they were most comfortable and I wore them for some considerable time, without I'm glad to say, having to use them for the purpose they were designed. When I was posted from Bomber Command in 1942 and joined a Coastal Command Sunderland squadron, they were much envied especially by our second pilot (Les Baveystock) who wished he'd had a similar pair when he was evading after being shot down during the first Thousand Bomber raid –1942.[2]

By this time Chas and I had successfully completed our conversion and having flown on air tests and training flights, we were eligible for crewing.

Chas was lucky joining a permanent crew, but I was put on the spare crew list and had to fly with any crew who were short of WOp/AG for one reason or another. This random crewing was similar to having to fly with pupils at the OTU – I recalled W/Cdr Snaith's cautionary comment about pushing one's luck by volunteering for a second tour!

However, for my first stand-in trip I flew with an experienced crew: S/Ldr Bouwen (Captain), Sgt Crowe (2nd pilot), F/O Brisbane (Nav/bomb-aimer), myself (1st

WOp/AG), Sgt Wilson (2nd WOp/AG), Sgt McFarlane (Flt/eng), and Sgt Moule (Tail-gunner). Our target was Stettin. Unfortunately on the way over the North Sea we lost an engine so we attacked an alternative target, the airfield at Aalborg in Denmark. I remembered it from my Whitley days as being well defended, and I was relieved when we bombed successfully and got back to base safely.

My next trip was with a different crew: Sgt Johnny Harwood (Captain), P/O McIntosh (2nd pilot), Sgt Scott (Nav/bomb-aimer), myself (1st WOp/AG), Sgt Patey (2nd WOp/AG), Sgt Bill Young (F/eng) and Sgt Reg Petch (Tail-gunner). Our task was to bomb the German warships *Scharnhorst* and *Gneisnau* at Brest (the *Scharnhorst* had been brought back to Brest after being damaged at La Rochelle). As always at Brest, the defences were formidable but we managed to bomb successfully, got through unscathed and back to base safely.

Another of my stand-in trips was with the same crew except that F/O Collins was Nav/bomb-aimer in place of Sgt Scott. Our target was shipping and dock installations at Hamburg. It turned out to be a flight I'll always remember! By this time in 1941, the Germans had improved and increased their anti-aircraft defences. Their night-fighters were not yet equipped with AI (Air-borne Interception) radar, but by using two types of ground radar, Freya and Wurzburg, ground controllers could vector a fighter to within 400 yards of a target. Also, the number of guns and searchlights had been increased to defend all major targets. What came to be known as the Kammhuber Defence Line, extending in depth from the Danish border to all the major industrial areas in the Ruhr, had also been established.

Nowadays, when reference is made to 'cones' it probably applies to ice-cream or roadworks! However, during the Second World War, the word was used in a different context. The mention of cones to bomber crews was likely to evoke the memory of their or some other unfortunate crew's aircraft caught in the apex of a cone of numerous searchlights, while associated flak batteries endeavoured to pound them to destruction, or hold them in the beams while a night-fighter stalked in for the kill – very few survived to tell the tale.

On the night in question, we took off in the early evening and set off for Hamburg. The weather conditions were good for a change and our flight across the North Sea passed without incident. Approaching the German coast, we carefully avoided the defences at Cuxhaven and followed the course of the River Elbe to Hamburg. Our Nav/bomb-aimer moved to his bombing position in the nose of the aircraft to set up his bomb-sight and guide us to the target. As we got near we could see considerable searchlight and flak activity, an indication that the attack was well under way.

At this time we were flying at 17,000 feet (the days of attacking from 4,000 feet were long gone, because by now even the light flak was reaching 12,000 feet). F/O Collins had identified the target and was preparing our run-in. Suddenly we were picked up in the beam of a blue searchlight, probably radar directed. It was immediately supported by many others and within seconds we were in the apex of a cone of blinding light. Johnny our skipper took immediate action to get us out of the cone as the flak burst near us. He flung the aircraft all over the sky, turning, diving and climbing, but unfortunately during one of these violent manoeuvres the aircraft stalled. Juddering, it hung on the props, then the nose dropped sickeningly and it plummeted downwards. During the transition from the nose-up to the nose-down attitude, dust arose from the floor in a cloud and loose objects such as maps, charts and logbooks were thrown about like confetti. Crew members who weren't strapped in held onto anything they could. Afterwards Bill Young (F/eng) told us that the accumulators had been wrenched from their mounting and were swinging on the leads!

In my position under the pilots' seats, I hung onto my seat with my right hand while I operated the IFF (Identification Friend or Foe) set with my left hand. There was a theory if you operated the IFF on the Broad/Distress band intermittently you could possibly give false indications to the radar controlling the searchlights. On this occasion it had no effect, except that operating it took my mind off the gravity of our situation. In predicaments such as this, crew members other that pilots can do little to quell their rising fears except hang on and pray, yes pray – I can tell you from experience that when the chips are down there aren't many unbelievers!

Maybe our combined pleas paid off, because Johnny and Mac, his co-pilot (a six-foot something sixteen-stone Aussie), got the aircraft under some semblance of control. By this time though we were down to 10,000 feet and still receiving the attentions of the searchlights and flak. There was nothing to be done except continue the violent evasive action, but in doing so we rapidly lost more height and we were soon passing through 5,000 feet. The situation was now desperate, so as a last resort the bombs were jettisoned as we continued diving towards the ground. Even as we did so the searchlights and flak attempted to follow us. We levelled off at roof-top height going like a bat out of hell. Finally we managed to escape from the defences and lost no time in getting out of the area. I don't think any of us regained our composure until we crossed the German coast and set course for base. The whole incident had only lasted a comparatively short time but it had seemed like a lifetime. Luckily the flak damage we had sustained wasn't serious and none of the crew had been hit. The rest of the flight back home was, thankfully, uneventful and we landed safely back at base.

We were transported to the Operations Block for debriefing and, as we entered, another crew (captained by P/O Hank Iveson) was completing their interrogation. We heard the IO ask them if they had anything further to report. One of them replied, 'Oh yes, we saw some poor sods getting a pasting over the target, the searchlights and flak even followed them down to deck level, it's very doubtful if they could have survived.' When our turn came to be debriefed, we were able to corroborate their statement, identifying ourselves as 'the poor sods being pasted over the target' and thankfully prove they were wrong in assuming we had bitten it!

However, the whole crew had been well and truly shaken by the episode. I suppose we were all feeling the effects of what is now referred to as post-traumatic stress, but in those days there were no counsellors to help us. For my part I was convinced that I'd had enough of being a stand-in so as soon as the opportunity presented itself, I requested the Flight Commander that I be attached to a permanent crew as soon as possible.

At this time the new postings to the squadron from the OTUs included Canadians, Australians and Kiwis. They were a great bunch of boys who had no inhibitions and their own ideas about discipline. To ease the accommodation limitations of the Sergeants' Mess, a manor house, Dinsdale Hall, was commandeered to house the squadron SNCO aircrew. The rooms were quite large, sparely furnished with the usual RAF type beds and lockers, but fairly comfortable. We had our own crew transport which took us to and from the aerodrome as required. We were given our main meals in the Sergeants' Mess, but there was also limited catering at the Hall which provided us with the odd cuppa and sandwiches.

We soon settled in and it wasn't long before our wild Colonial Boys introduced us to some aspects of their culture like craps (dice) and poker. Our pay being less than theirs meant we had to curb any tendency to over-indulge but we learnt fast and had the odd flutter. The village of Middleton-one-Row was within walking distance and the Davenport pub was soon adopted as a local watering hole. However the short cut from the Hall across country involved getting across the River Tees, using stepping-stones. The outbound journey when sober presented no problem but negotiating the stepping-stones on return late at night in a slightly unsteady state could cause difficulty. There were occasions when uniforms had to be draped across chairs in front of the Hall fires! We were also made welcome at the golf club at Dinsdale where we were kindly allowed to use their facilities. If we wanted to go further afield to the flesh pots of Darlington and Stockton we were allowed to use the crew transport to and from Dinsdale railway station.

One of the new boys was an Australian Sergeant Pilot, Keith Lloyd-Jones who was forming a new crew. When we struck up a friendship he asked me if I'd be his WOp/AG and after getting permission from the Flight Commander I joined the other crew members, P/O Bill Culmsee (2nd pilot) P/O Bob Fairclough (Nav/bomb-aimer), Sgt Batchelor (2nd WOp/AG), Sgt Phil Weeldon (F/eng), and Canadian Sgt Dickie Moule (Tail-gunner) with whom I'd flown previously. Although their operational experience was limited, all being on their first tour, they seemed to be well 'clued up' and after I'd flown with them on a few training flights, I considered I'd made the right decision.

We commenced operations as a new crew with a raid on the docks and submarine pens at St Nazaire on the night of the 7/8 January 1942. It turned out to be a successful debut. We bombed the target as briefed, got through the defences without suffering any damage or casualties and got back safely, very satisfied with our night's work.

Our next trip was to bomb an industrial complex at Mannheim on the River Rhine. My last trip there in a Whitley in 1940 to drop 'W' bombs in the Rhine had been a real hairy do and I hoped we'd be more fortunate this time. Although the opposition was severe everything went very well, we bombed and got a picture of the aiming point indicating a successful attack. We got back to base safely and the next night after our target photograph had been developed and assessed, we were invited to the Officers' Mess where the Station Commander, G/Capt T.C. (Tommy) Traill, congratulated us in the time-honoured fashion – thank you Sir, mine's a pint!

Because of adverse weather, there were some frustrating 'ops on, ops off' incidents, sometimes raids being cancelled at the last moment. On one such occasion we had a dramatic cancellation. 78 Squadron, still equipped with Whitleys, shared the airfield with us and when we operated together 78 would take-off before us.

On the night in question our crew was involved and as we were taxiing to the runway to follow the last of the Whitleys the incident occurred. One of the Whitleys aborted its take-off and stopped on the runway. There must have been a breakdown in communications because the next Whitley commenced its take-off run and ran into the stationary aircraft on the runway. Air Traffic ordered all aircraft on the ground to clear the area. We did an about turn (literally) and returned to dispersal, shut down and left the aircraft, smartly.

By this time the two fully-laden Whitleys on the runway had begun to burn and could go up at any time. Miraculously both crews were able to evacuate and get well away from their aircraft before this happened. When it did, a crater was blasted in the runway twenty feet deep and the width of the runway. When everything subsided a Merlin engine was found two hundred yards away.

After the runway had been repaired and the weather improved, we carried out our next bombing sortie against Cologne, where opposition was always severe. It proved to be so on this occasion. To make matters worse we had a couple of hiccups over the target. I'd left my radio position and was in the fuselage by the flare-chute giving Phil Weeldon our F/eng assistance to drop flares. Unfortunately one of them got stuck in the chute on its way out. The pin had been pulled so the flare was possibly live and there was a risk of it igniting in the chute. Taking a chance we grabbed another flare and used it to force the other flare down the chute and away from the aircraft before it went off – luckily we were successful. While Phil and I were having our excitement in the fuselage, the bods (pilots) up front were attempting to discover why the aircraft wasn't handling as it should. Their problem turned out to be self-inflicted. During evasive action the flaps had been inadvertently lowered, thus increasing the drag. However, the error was recognised and rectified – the handling and evasive action improved and we left the area safely and completed another successful sortie.

From time to time the squadron was the recipient of visits by top brass and VIPs, and in January 1942 HRH The Duke of Kent paid us a visit. He chatted to our crew in the squadron locker-room as we donned our flying kit prior to going flying. He gave the impression he was well clued up on the operational set-up.

On 12 February the German battlecruisers *Scharnhorst* and *Gneisnau*, making use of the bad weather and low cloud, escaped from Brest and got through the straits of Dover to the safety of German ports. Our squadron with others was involved in an attempt to intercept and attack them but because of the weather conditions we were unsuccessful.

This turned out to be my last trip with the crew and the squadron because at the end of February, Chas Armstrong and myself were posted back to the Electrical and Wireless School at Cranwell to remuster to WOM/AG (Wireless Operator Mechanic/Air-gunner). Although I hadn't flown with the crew long I was sorry to leave them and the squadron. We made our farewells and promised to keep in touch.

When we got to Cranwell we joined other ex-operational WOp/AGs from Bomber Command who like ourselves were remustering. One of them, Howard Webb, was an ex-Blenheim boy with the DFM and Bar, while another, 'Brum' Madkins was a real old sweat having completed a pre-war overseas tour on the North West Frontier of India flying in Wapitis against the recalcitrant natives – he still carried his 'Goli (Goolie) chit'. At the outbreak of war he was serving with a Fairey Battle Squadron which was sent to France as part of the AASF. During the Battle of France he was shot down, but walked back to base and eventually returned to the UK, where he finished his tour on Wellingtons. He was a marvellous character who hadn't even been mentioned in Dispatches.

At the end of March, I had a phone call from Keith, my wild colonial ex-skipper informing me that he'd been commissioned and that I'd been awarded a 'gong', the DFM (Distinguished Flying Medal). He told me that he and the crew were looking forward to celebrating both when I returned to the squadron, and in typical 'Strine' he said, 'And it will be your turn to kick the tin sport', inferring I would have to pay! Sadly those were the last words he spoke to me because on the night of the 12/13 April 1942, the crew was shot down during a raid an Essen. He and five other members of the crew were killed. Only Bob Fairclough (navigator) survived and was made prisoner. The six who perished were buried at Gelsenkirchen. They are now buried in the Allied War Graves Cemetery in the Reichswald Forest near Kleve in West Germany, where over 6,000 Allied personnel, mostly Bomber Command aircrew in their early twenties and younger, are buried.[3]

By the middle of May we had successfully completed our course remustering to WOM and returned to our units to await developments. When Chas and I returned to 76 Squadron at Middleton-St-George the Adjutant advised us that as we were now WOM/AGs our posting to Coastal Command was pending and to take the opportunity of going on leave. This worked out very well because while we had been at Cranwell, Chas' fiancee's family had been making preparations for their daughter and Chas' wedding. Chas paid me the compliment of asking me to be his best man. The wedding took place as planned and he and his bride were able to take an uninterrupted honeymoon.

It was while we were on leave that Air Marshal Harris launched the first successful Thousand Bomber raids, proving that his plan for all-out mass bombing was viable and could be a decisive factor to bring about the defeat of Germany.

However on 22 June, he lost two of his stalwart supporting aircrew as Chas and myself were posted to 1447 Flight at RAF Hooton Park, to carry out preliminary training before proceeding to the Sunderland OTU at RAF Invergordon, for conversion and crewing.

Notes

1 The Bickford saga doesn't end there. Fifty-two years later I received a telephone call from Richard Bickford Jr who was only eight weeks old when his father was killed. He had traced me through my book, *The Whitley Boys* in which I describe the raids during 1939/40 when I flew with his father as his tail-gunner.

The outcome was that I visited him at his home, met his family and had a long conversation during which I recalled the time I flew with his father. I was able to provide missing details concerning his father's career on the squadrons in which we'd served, and give him some memorabilia of that period.

Richard Jr was also a flier, having served as a helicopter pilot with the Royal Navy. On leaving the Navy he became a commercial pilot and at the time I met him, he was a senior captain flying with British Airways. During our conversation he suggested we make history repeat itself – as I'd flown with the father, I should now fly with the son! He arranged for me to fly with him on a round trip to Rome. This turned out to be a wonderful experience during which I sat in the cockpit with him and attempted to absorb the present day flying technique and technology. It was a far cry from when we groped our way around Europe during 1939/40 at night in our primitive aircraft using Dead Reckoning navigation, because of the lack of other suitable aids. We remain in contact and are good friends.

2 See Chapter Eight.

3 A few years ago I made a pilgrimage to Reichswald to pay my respects. On my way from Amsterdam by train to Nijmegen I got into conversation with some Dutch fellow passengers. One of them was a lady also going to Nijmegen, where she lived and practised as a lawyer, as well as being a city councillor.

When we arrived at Nijmegen she escorted me to the bus station where I hoped to get a bus to Kleve, then a taxi to Reichswald. On consulting the timetable she told me that I'd just missed the bus and there wouldn't be another for three hours. This meant that I would have to go by taxi because I had to get back to Amsterdam from where I was leaving the following morning to return to the UK. When I told the lady of my intentions, she asked me to wait for a few minutes. She left me and returned after a short while in a car with a driver. She instructed him to take me to Reichswald and bring me back to the station. I protested that I couldn't accept such generosity, but she cut me short insisting that it was nothing compared with what the Royal Air Force had done for the Dutch people during the war.

With my faith in man and womankind renewed and feeling very humble, I was driven to Reichswald where I paid my respects. As I stood by the graves of my crew I was haunted by the innate guilt of most survivors, 'Why them and not me?'

My Halifax crew shot down over Essen-42.

Handley-Page Halifax Mark IIs.

Handley-Page Halifax Mark I.

P/O Lloyd-Jones' grave in the Reichswald Forest War Graves Cemetery.

Eight
Coastal Command
Here We Come

Chas and I reported to 1447 Flight RAF Hooton Park and we spent two months flying Oxfords on a pre-OTU course, before proceeding to the Coastal Command OTU at Invergordon to convert onto Sunderland flying-boats. Some of the other Bomber Command 'exiles' with whom we'd worked at Cranwell on the remustering course were also there. After completing our pre-OTU course we left Hooton-Park for Invergardon, where we started the boat course.

To we ex-bomber land-lubbers, the Sunderland was quite a change and we were all impressed by its qualities, it was roomy – enormous compared with the aircraft we'd flown in Bomber Command and it was quite something to be able to get around in it without bending double. It seemed to handle well, was fairly well armed and had facilities (a flush toilet – the height of luxury) which we Bomber 'peasants' didn't realise existed in aircraft. It also had a galley/kitchen with cooking facilities, and a wardroom with dining and rest facilities – what more could you ask for? This was the way to fight a war! Mind you there were snags – more than one ex-bomber land-lubber found to his cost when he forgot where he was and stepped from a hatch into the oggin! However we soon got our sea legs, learning how to handle sea-drogues and how to moor up to buoys in choppy conditions. The flying was also quite a change, no more high altitude stuff breathing oxygen for hours on end and no parachute harnesses to wear, only Mae Wests. All things considered, I now know why the postings to flying-boat squadrons in peacetime were sought after. The Sunderland soon became one of my favourite aircraft.

Our conversion course proceeded as planned. I trained with an all-Australian crew and we got on very well, despite them referring to me as that Pom so and so from time to time!

We had with us on the course S/Ldr B.P. Young (later Air Vice-Marshal) who was returning to operational flying after recovering from serious burn injuries suffered when he was shot down while flying Hurricanes during the Battle of France in 1940. He proved to be very popular and during the course was to gain some good-natured notoriety when he and his U/T crew inadvertently depth-charged a whale, mistaking it for a U-boat during one of their operational training sorties ever the North Atlantic.

On the successful completion of the conversion course I was pleased to learn that I was to join No. 461 RAAF (Royal Australian Air Force) Squadron at RAF Hamworthy near Poole in Dorset, with the rest of my Aussie crew. Having got on very well with Keith my

Aussie skipper in Bomber Command, I looked forward to meeting and flying with other boys from down under. It meant however parting company with my oppo Chas Armstrong, as he was posted with S/Ldr Young to a new squadron being formed at RAF Bowmore, in the Inner Hebrides, but we we'd get together again on many occasions in the future.

In 1939, before the outbreak of war, regular aircrew and ground crew of No. 10 Royal Australian Air Force, came to England to convert onto Sunderland flying boats, then fly them back to Australia. However, this was thwarted when Britain declared war on Germany on 3 September 1939. It was mutually agreed by the British and Australian Governments that No. 10 Squadron should stay in the UK and fly with Coastal Command. From the outset the squadron did sterling work carrying out anti-submarine and convoy protection patrols.

As the war progressed, a stream of Australian reinforcements arrived in the UK and in 1942 it was decided to form another Australian flying boat squadron, with a nucleus of experienced aircrew and ground crew from No. 10 RAAF Squadron, supplemented with the Australian reinforcements. However, although there were enough Australian pilots, navigators, WOp/AGs and AGs, there weren't enough flight-engineers and practically no WOM/AGs. To overcome this deficit, RAF flight-engineers and WOM/AGs were posted to the newly-formed squadron, No. 461, based at RAF Hamworthy, near Poole.

When I arrived at the squadron, I was barely given time to book in, before I was summoned to the Adjutant's office. He informed me instructions had been received to the effect that I was to attend an investiture at Buckingham Palace in three days time to collect my DFM. His actual words were, 'You're due at Buck House in three days time to get your gong sport, so you'd better get cracking.' I got cracking immediately, arranging for invitations to be sent to my parents to attend the ceremony, as well as sending them an explanatory 'greetings' telegram to avoid arousing any misgivings.

On the morning of the big day, I caught a very early train to London to ensure I would arrive with time to spare. During the journey I think I must have re-polished my buttons and shoes over and over again to make sure I was presentable. The journey went smoothly until we reached the outskirts of the city, when the train was held up. Apparently during the night the track had been damaged during an air raid. Panic stations – I contacted the train guard and asked him how long we were likely to be delayed, explaining the cause of my anxiety. He reassured me that it wouldn't be long before we were on our way again, so muttering my prayers, I returned to my carriage. As the minutes ticked by I was sure I wasn't going to get to the palace on time. However, someone up there must have heard me and we got on our way, but once we reached Waterloo Station time was getting short.

I left the carriage on the run and tore through the station to the taxi rank only to find the usual wartime queue. Fortunately there was an elderly special policeman nearby. I approached him and told him of my predicament. His reaction was immediate, 'Don't worry son, come with me,' and he led me to the head of the queue ignoring the catcalls from the other waiting passengers, opened the door of the leading taxi, heaved me in the back and yelled to the startled driver, 'To the palace, and don't spare the horses!'

The driver let out the clutch and we left the station with tyres smoking. As I settled in my seat, the driver with typical Cockney humour said, 'Alright mate, which palace –

Regent, Strand or Buckingham?' The two former being well-known hotels. When I informed him it was Buckingham and that I was attending an Investiture, that is if he could get me there in time, he replied, 'Don't worry cock, hang onto your hat, we can't keep His Majesty waitin' can we?' True to his word he got me there with time to spare and as I attempted to pay him, he said, 'Have this one on me son and give 'is Majesty my regards!'

My parents were waiting for me at the Palace gates, through which we were allowed to proceed after having our identification checked. Inside the gates we split up, my parents being directed to the Public Viewing Gallery in the Investiture room and myself to a cloakroom where I deposited my cap, gas-mask and steel helmet. I was then directed to a large room where award recipients were gathering. They were all members of the three services, Navy, Army and Air Force. Chas Armstrong's name had appeared in the same issue of the *London Gazette*, so I assumed it was likely he would be attending the same Investiture. He was – I spotted him and we were soon chewing the fat and catching up with each other's news.

During wartime there were two classes of Investiture, one for commissioned ranks, recipients of Orders and Crosses and another for non-commissioned ranks, recipients of medals. This Investiture was in this latter category. We were all milling around chatting when our attention was diverted by the entrance of a very presentable young man. He had blonde curling hair and he was dressed in a black morning coat with a flower in the buttonhole, pin-striped trousers, a grey cravat and black patent leather shoes. He came to the centre of the room and called for attention, then in a cut glass accent, announced, 'I want DSMs over thar, DCMs over thar and DFMs over thar.' As we moved to where he had indicated, a very large sailor commented in a stage whisper, 'Gawd, if the Germans get to 'im, they won't want to fight 'im, will they!' Eventually when we were all assembled in our award groups and our names confirmed on his list, his assistants placed a small hook on the ribbon of the medal we were to receive. When this was done to his satisfaction, he and his assistants left the room.

He was replaced by a fierce-looking elderly naval officer whose uniform was covered with gold braid and fruit salad (medal ribbons). He stumped to the centre of the room and addressed us. 'Before you leave this room you will be assembled in alphabetical order. When the time comes for the Investiture to commence, the doors behind me will open and you will file slowly through them and walk along the carpeted corridor to the Investiture area where the Monarch and his entourage are waiting. As you approach the area, you will see a small white triangle marked on the carpet and as your name and decoration is announced, you will advance onto the triangle and halt – don't stamp your feet! You will then turn left towards His Majesty, bow and take two steps towards him and halt. He will then present you with your decoration, placing it on the hook on your ribbon. He will also congratulate you and shake your hand – don't grip tightly. You will then take two steps backward onto the white triangle, bow, turn right and leave the room via the corridor. On leaving, report to the two Yeomen of the Guard seated at a table on your right. They will remove your decoration and place it in a box with your name on it. You can then leave the palace if you wish, however your parents/friends will not be able to leave until all the recipients have received their awards.' He finished his briefing with a menacing, 'Any questions?' There were none, so he left the room and the black-coated gentlemen with his assistants reappeared to line us up in alphabetical order in single file.

At the appointed time the doors opened to the Investiture Room and we filed slowly through to the muted music from a military orchestra. Chas and myself having names with letters at the beginning of the alphabet were up near the front of the file. As we moved along I managed to locate my parents who were seated in the gallery facing the investiture area.

Immediately in front of me was the large sailor who had made the remark about the frock-coated gentleman. As his name was called he stepped onto the white triangle as briefed, but from then on he did his own thing. He did what can only be described as a rate four (steep) turn to the left and took two steps towards His Majesty over whom he literally towered. The King looked up at him, placed the decoration on the hook shook his hand and congratulated him. Our mariner stepped back onto the white triangle, did a right turn and was about to march off when he remembered he hadn't bowed. His recovery action was a quick nod over his left shoulder. His performance had nearly put paid to my efforts to remember and carry out the correct procedure, but I managed it as briefed and my chest measurement increased by a couple of inches as His Majesty hooked on my medal, said 'Well done' and shook my hand. I then carried out the departure procedure as instructed and left the room.

Chas was waiting for me by the table where the two Yeomen of the Guard sat. One of them took my medal off the hook and placed it in a small white cardboard box with my name written on it. Apparently only Orders and Crosses merited silk-lined monogrammed cases. We asked the Yeomen how long they estimated the investiture would last and one of the replied, 'There's not many of you this morning, so it should be all over in about another hour and a half. If you want you can leave now and come back for your friends later. There's a pub called the Bag of Nails along the Palace Mews where you can get a drink if you are so inclined.' It seemed like a good suggestion, so we collected our caps etc. and left the palace.

Following the Yeomen's directions we found the Bag of Nails and entered the bar. The mariner was already there celebrating with his friends. The landlord greeted us, 'Morning, what can I get you ruddy 'eroes?' We got our drinks and sat down. The Navy invited us to join them, but we resisted.

It looked like a thrash could develop but as we didn't want to keep our parents waiting, we had our drink, and left again for the palace. When we got there our parents were just leaving and as we met them we were joined by photographers from our local newspapers wanting pictures of their local boys, With all due modesty we posed as requested, then after chatting for a while took our leave and went on our respective ways.

My parents and I went to the hotel at which we had arranged to stay (neither the Strand nor Regent Palace!) and that evening had a celebration to mark what had been one of our most memorable days. Nowadays whenever I go to London, I recall that wonderful day when the kindly policeman threw me into a taxi and shouted 'To the palace!'

When I got back to Hamworthy the day following the investiture, I found that our Invergordon crew had been split up and I had been selected to join a new crew being formed, captained by F/O Dudley Marrows. The other members were, P/O Jock Rolland navigator, myself as WOM/AG, P/O Pete Jensen WOp/AG, Sgt Dusty Miller WOp/AG, Sgt Lance Woodland F/eng, Sgt 'Bubbles' Pearce flight mechanic (the 'Bubbles' was because of his rotundity and personality), Sgt Frank (Pierre) Bamber flight/rigger (Pierre because of his Gallic appearance), and Sgt Bunny Sidney tail-gunner. The second pilot slot was initially filled by P/O Keith Carmody (who made a name for himself in Australian state cricket after the war) or Sgt Jack Tamsett, until Sgt Les Baveystock DFM, another Bomber Command exile joined us.

We started our crew get together training by being sent to RAF Pembroke Dock, near Milford Haven in South Wales, to carry out a concentrated session of armament training before being sent on active operations. This training comprised air-to-sea firing, fighter affiliation with one of the locally based Spitfire squadrons and low-level bombing (simulated depth-charge) attacks on targets in Angle Bay. The air-firing and the fighter affiliation exercises were carried out successfully, but during one of the bombing sorties we had a slight 'hiccup'.

In the Sunderland, bombs/depth-charges were carried internally on racks in the large bomb compartment, which was aft of the ward-room and kitchen/galley. When required, the two bomb-doors, one on each side of the bomb-room were pulled down internally to allow the bomb/depth-charges to run out along the rails fixed under each wing. This was controlled from an electrical panel on the bomb-door bulkhead by one of the two crew members detailed to act as bomb-reloaders.

For practice purposes, small smoke bombs were attached to the Universal bomb carriers by means of a device known as the Garner adapter, which wasn't as efficient as it might have been and unfortunately during some bomb releases bombs were left 'hung up' on the racks. There were two recognised corrective measures. In the case of a 'hang up' on the inner racks, the bomb could be knocked off by one of the re-loading crew leaning out of the open bomb-doors wielding a boat-hook. If the 'hang up' occurred on one of the outer racks, the procedure was to retract the rack along the rails and as it came within reach to lean out and grab the bomb, that is if it hadn't fallen off on the way in.

For this sortie Jock and Bubbles were detailed as reloaders. This was because they were both prone to air-sickness, so the only place they could be usefully employed was in the bomb-room where they had quick access to the john if it became necessary for them to part with their breakfasts! While we were making one of our final bomb-runs, the event that reloaders dreaded occurred – a hang-up on one of the outer racks. Bubbles operated the control to retract the rack, while Jock positioned himself by the open bomb-door to grab the hung-up bomb from the rack as it came within reach. That was the plan, but when the bomb was a couple of inches from Jock's outstretched fingers, it dropped free. A quick glance downwards showed Jock we were still flying over water as the bomb proceeded on its downward path, but the sea gave way to the shore-line and to his horror, the back garden of a house came into view where the housewife had recently hung out her washing to dry! He watched the rogue bomb fly over the fence to the far side of the garden where it exploded, engulfing everything in white smoke.

He immediately informed Dudley what had happened and got his ear bent for not reporting the hang-up earlier. We circled the house until the smoke dispersed and were very relieved to see that apparently no damage or injury had been caused, that is apart from smoking the laundry!

When we landed at Pembroke Dock, the incident had been reported, but luckily for us other aircraft had been on the bombing-range at the same time as ourselves, so although we were suspected as being the culprits, the powers that be couldn't be certain. As we were just about finishing the course and keen to return to Hamworthy, Dudley hedged his bets, crossed his fingers and kept mum. Grudgingly they gave us the benefit of the doubt. Before returning to Hamworthy we made sure that the unfortunate housewife whose laundry we'd smoked was suitably compensated. However like the Ancient Mariner, we were lumbered by this Albatross from then on. On future occasions when we were diverted to Pembroke Dock, the Station Commander inevitably steered the chat to smoke-bombs in back gardens!

On return to Hamworthy our crew was put on the 'readiness' list for operations and a couple of days later on 20 November 1942 we were detailed for our first operational sortie, an anti-sub patrol to look for and attack U-boats in the Bay of Biscay on their way to and from the German occupied French ports. Our search, which lasted over twelve hours, was unfortunately fruitless. However, the Squadron Commander (W/Cdr Lovelock) who flew with us as check pilot must have been satisfied with our performance because from then on we were officially operational.

Throughout November and December 1942 we continued our anti-submarine patrols over the Bay of Biscay plus a couple of convoy protection patrols. It was during one of these convoy patrols in the Western Approaches that we were reminded of the hardships and risks the Merchant and Royal Navy boys had to endure. As we flew around the convoy which was escorted by destroyers and corvettes, we marvelled as the ships porpoised in the towering seas. It must have been hellish for the crews and it made us

The crew of Sunderland U-461 Squadron. Left to right, standing: Sgt Bunny Sidney, F/O Dudley Marrows, Sgt Les Baveystock DFM, Sgt 'Bubbles' Pierce, Sgt 'Pierre' Bamber, Sgt Lance Woodland, F/Sgt Larry Donnelly DFM. Seated: Sgt 'Dusty' Miller, P/O Jock Rolland, P/O Pete Jensen.

Larry Donnelly at the wireless position in a Sunderland.

Short Sunderland.

humbly grateful for our comparative wellbeing. What a debt we owe them!

By this time the crew were working well together and I appreciated the fact that Les Baveystock was now with us, because I now had a fellow Pom to help me keep my end up with the rest of our wild colonial crew. During the many conversations I had with him he was very reluctant to talk about his time in Bomber Command, apart from telling me he had flown Hampdens at an OTU before being posted to a Manchester squadron. He explained his reticence much later in 1987 when I attended a Sunderland reunion in Australia. We spent a week together during which he told me about his brief but remarkable career in Bomber Command. After I'd learned what had happened I assisted him to write the following account.

Les Baveystock's Story

I was just one month off my twenty-sixth birthday and had been married for two and a half years, when I joined the RAFVR in early October 1940. After completing ITW at Newquay, followed by EFTS at Staverton on Tiger Moths, I went to Canada where at 34 SFTS, Medicine Hat, I qualified as Sergeant Pilot on Oxfords.

Returning to the UK, I was posted to 14 (Hampden) OTU Cottesmore, and soon discovered the difficulties of night flying in the black-out after flying in Canada, where everything was lit up. That problem and the inherent 'stabilised' yaw to which Hampdens were prone when coming in to land with U/C and flaps down, caused me some anxious moments. The casualty rate was high, five out of the sixteen pilots and their WOp/AGs on my course were killed in crashes.

My morale hit zero when I was detailed as one of the pall-bearers to a young Pilot Officer, who we buried in Cottesmore cemetery. As we marched back to the station another one of the pall-bearers, a Sergeant Pilot remarked to me: 'Well Bav, we now know what will happen when our turn comes, don't we?' Exactly one week later, I helped carry his coffin after he had become another crash victim.

I survived OTU and was posted to No. 50 Squadron at Skellingthorpe, but to my horror I found they were flying the ill-fated Manchesters – out of the frying-pan into the fire! After two local flights with different pilots I went as second pilot to a Sgt Gruber to bomb the Heinkel Works at Rostock. I had received no instruction on Manchesters and the only information I had obtained about the aircraft, was that which I had gleaned myself. Two nights later we did another raid on Rostock. I did two more ops and some local flying before I was given my first dual instruction on the aircraft – it lasted fifty minutes. A few days later I had another fifty minutes dual, followed by what was to be my only solo on type – it lasted ten minutes! I did more local flights as second pilot and was then sent on a BAT (Blind Flying) course at Waddington.

I returned to Skellingthorpe where preparations were in progress for what was to be the first Thousand Bomber Raid, and to find I'd been crewed to fly as second 'Dickey' to F/O Manser. Up to then I hadn't met him or the other members of his crew. By the morning of 30 May fifteen aircraft and crews were listed on the squadron notice-board, but ours wasn't among them. However, later that morning, we were called to the Flight Office with another crew and detailed to go to Conningsby and bring back two Manchesters which we would fly that night.

I had been given a weekend pass and Betty, my wife, was coming to Lincoln to spend it with me. It was now too late to stop her, so I asked that instead of going to Conningsby I be allowed to go and meet her. I was given permission but warned not to say anything about the forthcoming raid. So while I went to Lincoln, Manser and the rest of the crew went to Conningsby where they collected the Manchester, which turned out to be one relegated to circuit and bumps training. It had no mid-upper turret and the auto-pilot was U/S – not the ideal aircraft to fly on operations.

We got off on schedule and started to climb on course. When we reached Cologne we started a long run-in at 7,000 feet. We were picked up by search-lights and the flak came up thick and fast, but Manser held the aircraft straight and level until the 'bombs gone' call. The bombs must have just left the aircraft when we received a direct hit. Manser thrust the stick forward diving and turning the aircraft to escape from the hail of flak coming at us. I hung on grimly as we finally escaped into the darkness, but by this time we were down to 800 feet and the fuselage was full of smoke. Naylor, the tail-gunner yelled he'd been hit. Manser told him to hang on while we found out what was on fire. We suspected that some of the incendiaries had hung-up and been hit.

I went back to the fuselage with the WOp/AG and wrenched the cover off the forward end of the bomb-bay. Everything looked normal, but when we looked into the rear end we were looking straight through to the ground. The rear part of the bomb-doors had been blown off, but fortunately all the bombs had gone and nothing seemed to be burning.

Returning to the cockpit I found Manser attempting to climb the aircraft on full power to get more height in case we had to bale out. He had got it up to 2,000 feet when suddenly there was a 'whoomph' and the port engine burst into flames. On his order I turned off the petrol, feathered the prop, and activated the fire extinguisher. At first it had little effect and the flames streaked back over the wing past the breather on the port main petrol tank. I expected the bloody lot to go up, but gradually the flames died down. While Manser struggled to hold the aircraft on course (we were heading for Manston our nearest landfall) he sent me back to jettison everything I could saying, 'I doubt whether we'll make Manston, but we might make the Channel and ditch.'

Going to the fuselage I saw that by now, Bob Horsley (WOp/AG) had got Naylor the rear-gunner onto the rest-bed and was bandaging his wounds. I started jettisoning everything moveable down the flare-chute. First to go were the two VGOs and a dozen pans of ammunition which a well-meaning armourer, who seeing we had no mid-upper turret, had placed in the fuselage, under the mistaken idea we could use them if we were attacked – he meant well! The flares followed and I then started on the oxygen bottles.

Meanwhile up front, Manser was finding it impossible to keep the aircraft on course and maintain height. The starboard engine was now over-heating and might catch fire at any time. He concluded our only chance lay in baling out so he gave the order to abandon. Neither Horsley or myself were on intercom at the time, but luckily Horsley had plugged the wounded tail-gunner into the rest-bed intercom position. Although he was feeling the effects of a morphine injection, he heard the order and passed it on to us.

While Horsley helped the tail-gunner to the fuselage door, I went back to the cockpit in time to see the front-gunner Sgt Mills and the navigator F/O Barnes leaving from the front hatch. I glanced at the altimeter to see it reading 800 feet. The aircraft was juddering as it approached the stall as I quickly removed mine and Manser's parachutes from their stowage. Clipping on mine I leaned across Manser to fit his. Knowing full well if he let go of the controls the aircraft would flip over on its back, he turned to me and knocking his chute aside screamed to me, 'For God's sake, get out, we're going in'.

I crawled to the front hatch, doubled up and went out head-first pulling the rip-cord as I did so – there was no time to count because I was so low I could see the hedgerows in the moonlight. What can only have been seconds later, I plunged into a dyke full of water which broke my fall. The aircraft hit the ground and blew up not far from where I landed. Releasing my chute and harness I struggled to the dyke bank and attempted unsuccessfully to hide it under an over-hanging tree. By the time I'd scrambled out of the ditch the aircraft, which had fallen among some small trees, was engulfed in flames and the ammo was exploding in all directions. It was impossible to get near it and I knew Manser couldn't have survived.

Knowing when he gave the order to abandon that he had a wounded man on board and possibly two members not on intercom, he had deliberately held on to give everyone the maximum opportunity to get out – in doing so he sacrificed his own life.

I dumped my Mae West in the dyke and headed in a westerly direction getting my bearings from the Pole star. I was wearing the usual aircrew clobber, long johns, thick roll-neck sweater, battle-dress and fleece-lined flying boots, all completely sodden from my immersion in the dyke. The going was very heavy and my progress across the paddocks was hindered as I looked for gates/gaps in the hedges.

By now the fear I'd experienced when we were getting clobbered over Cologne followed by the engine fire and the shock of bailing out, were beginning to subside and I was able to take stock. On the credit side I was alive and miraculously uninjured, but apart from a knife and a handkerchief, I had nothing. Usually we were each issued an escape-kit containing maps, compasses, plus money of the countries over which we flew, but because we'd put up so many aircraft there wasn't enough to go round, we'd only been given three between us. So instead of distributing them, they'd all gone into the navigator's bag which had gone down with the aircraft. We'd been briefed to head for Gibraltar if we were shot down – in the circumstances, the thought of having to hike that distance was extremely daunting.

However I struggled on. As I entered one of the small paddocks I spotted a figure in the moonlight. I froze, thinking it was a German searching for us. After a few moments, which seemed a life-time, a voice called out in English 'Who's that?' Without thinking I replied, 'It's me Les Baveystock', and ran over to discover our second WOp/AG, Stan King. The relief was such we danced around like lunatics.

After our elation subsided we set off together but didn't make much progress because Stan had ricked his ankle on landing. As dawn broke we hid in the middle of a cornfield. The ground was completely water-logged and I was soaked. I hoped the sun would come out and I would be able to dry off, but instead it started to rain and I was wracked with cramps.

It was Sunday and we could hear church-bells ringing. I thought we might have reached Holland before the crash, but I wasn't sure (we were to learn later that the aircraft had crashed near the small Belgian village of Bree near the Dutch border). During the morning we saw a young boy herding cows in the next paddock and taking the risk we spoke to him and as he seemed quite friendly we headed for the farm nearby. Our luck was in. The farmer and his family, who were called Nijskens, took us inside and fed us, dried our clothes, then hid us in one of their haystacks while they contacted the local doctor whom they knew to be a member of the Belgian Resistance.

The next day they brought us into the farmhouse. At about 10 p.m. a young couple arrived. With them, to our surprise, was our 1st WOp/AG, Bob Horsley. They had brought bicycles for us and we all set off together in the dark. We were taken to a grain-mill at a place called Dilsen, which seemed to be a staging-post on the 'Escape Line'. There were several people there and we met a young woman named Gertrude Moors and a Dutchman named Armand Leviticus. He was also on the run from the Germans. I was still wearing my RAF battle-dress and a raincoat and clogs given to me by the Nijskens. Armand was carrying a suitcase full of clothes from which he produced a suit and offered it to me. At the time I didn't think it strange when he asked me to keep it and said he would collect it from me, if and when we got back to England. Events after the war were to prove otherwise.

At dawn the following morning we left Dilsen, Armand acting as my guide while Horsley and King went with Gertrude Moors. We travelled separately to Liege where Armand took me to a friend, Guus Oderkerken, who gave us breakfast. From there we went to the church of St Denis, arriving there at 10 a.m. as we'd been instructed to do. When we got inside we found that Gertrude Moors, Horsley and King already there. We went to the opposite side of the church and sat down.

We thought that the priest might be our contact, but he gave no indication and after a while, feeling something had gone wrong, Armand decided we should leave even though he hadn't a clue where to go. The others had been watching us and as we got up to leave, they did likewise and being closer to the door got out first.

As we mingled with the crowd outside, we were all picked up singly by several men acting independently. My unknown guide and I followed another man (who I later found out was the Police Chief of District 7 in Liege). He took us to a terraced house in the suburbs where we found Gertrude Moors, Horsley and King who had been joined by two other members of our crew, Sgts Mills and Naylor. The only one missing was F/O Barnes, our navigator (we were to find out later that he'd been injured on landing and had been captured by the Germans).

It was now 11 a.m. Tuesday. Having baled out at approximately 2 a.m. Sunday near the Belgian/Dutch border, it was difficult to realise we were now many miles away in Liege. We thanked our lucky stars we'd had the good fortune to have been picked up so quickly by the Resistance, who had spirited us out from under the noses of the Germans and fed us into their Escape Line.

We stayed in Liege for three days and nights, then left by train for Brussels. Armand Leviticus didn't come with us because they were giving us priority.

Before we left the house in Liege we thanked him for his help. He reminded me to keep his suit for him. I was never to see him again.

Bob Horsley and I were in one part of the train, while King, Mills and Naylor were in the other. We had all been given newspapers and briefed to pretend to read them throughout the journey and to avoid any attempts at conversation with the other passengers. Unlike English passengers who usually ignore each other, these Continentals gabbled away among themselves irrespective whether they knew each other or not.

Despite this we managed to arrive safely in Brussels. We had been briefed to leave the train with our newspapers rolled up under our arms. As we did so Bob and I were picked up by a lovely girl named Giselle Evrard who took us to her home in the Palace of Justice apartments where she lived with her parents and elderly grandma. The others, King, Naylor and Mills were in another apartment in the same building, having been taken there by a young man named Henri Steinbeck. We stayed in the apartments for five days, during which time we met other members of the Resistance and were given false identity documents and names. Mine was Van Ollebecke.

The next stage of the journey was to be by train from Brussels to Paris. As none of us spoke French or Flemish it was considered too dangerous for us to board the train in the main station in Brussels, so our guides took us on a local train to Lueven, east of Brussels where we would be able to intercept the Paris train in comparative safety. Our guide for this stage was a pretty little seventeen-year-old girl named Andree Dumont, whose Resistance codename was 'Nadine'.

When the Paris express arrived, Bob and I followed Nadine into the last carriage. To our dismay it was full of German soldiers en route for Paris and we had to make our way past them to get to the front carriage, which the Germans reserved for civilians as an anti-sabotage measure. On my way I accidentally bumped into one of the soldiers who grabbed me and yelled something in German. I thought my number was up as I hung my head and mumbled what I hoped he would accept as an apology. Luckily it seemed to satisfy him because he released me and I followed the other two to the front carriage where we found seats and settled in.

The train staged through Brussels where our compartment was filled with a lot of local people who not only seemed to know each other, but also seemed part of a gang. I was sitting near the corridor with Nadine who had Bob on the other side of her. She had instructed us to feign sleep, which we did, but some of the locals seemed suspicious of us and asked if we were travelling with her. She said we were and the reason we were tired was that we'd been travelling for many nights. This seemed to satisfy them. She told us later that they were most probably black marketeers on their way to Paris to further their under the counter activities.

The train crossed the French border where we had to disembark for an identity check. Our false documents saw us through, but when we reboarded the train we found our seats had been taken and we spent the rest of the journey huddled in the corridor. We arrived in Paris at about 6 a.m. and after getting us through the checkpoint, Nadine took us to a small café where we had a cup of ersatz coffee. She then took us to our next pick-up point at one of the Metro stations and handed us over to our new guide, an attractive older girl named Andree de Jongh, who turned out to be the leader and founder of the 'Comete' Escape Line. After a brief farewell, Nadine left us to return to Brussels. Andree (Dede) de Jongh took us to a house in Paris where she shared a flat with another girl. They gave us breakfast and left to obtain new identity and travel documents for us.

When they came back I found that my new name was to be (you'd better believe it) Jean Thomas! Dede had brought back with her another member of the Comete Line organisation, a girl called Elvire Morelle. She walked with a limp having suffered a broken leg during one of her crossings of the Pyrenees – she had been carried out on her guide's back! They then took us to a restaurant where we met Elvire's brother Charlie. He had with him a young Canadian airman named Hal Demone and a young Belgian who like us, were on the Escape Line back to England.

The next and longest stage of our journey was by train from Paris to Bayanne near the Franco/Spanish border. We had to pass through the restricted zone of Western France, but we carried special passes and a letter from the Mayor of Bayonne stating we were required for municipal duties with the local council. They were of course, all forged, but were over-stamped with a stolen German seal. We were accompanied by Dede de Jongh and our journey passed without incident, but there were times of severe strain when we came under scrutiny.

When the train reached Bayonne, Hal Demone and the young Belgian were taken off the train and handed over to Madame de Greef (codenamed 'Tante Go') and her daughter Janine. Bob and I stayed with Dede until the train reached St Jean de Luz, where we disembarked. I was now wearing a beret and a continental style suit, so taking the risk my appearance and false documents would convince the Germans I was a local Basque, I went through the checkpoint. It worked – I think my big hooter helped! Bob however, had blue eyes and stood out like a sore thumb, so he hid in the toilet on the train until all the other passengers had disembarked, then left discreetly and got through a gate to rejoin Dede and myself.

Dede then took us to another safe house in St Jean de Luz, where we stayed for three days. On the third day at about 6 p.m. we left, following Dede from a safe distance. She took us to a farmhouse at Urrgne in the foothills of the Pyrenees, owned by a middle-aged lady named Francoise Usandizaga. There we met our Basque guide Florentino and set off on what proved to be the most arduous journey I've ever made. The distance to Rentaria in Spain directly was twenty-two kilometres, but climbing, descending and deviations made it much longer. By the time we reached our destination, ten hours later, we were exhausted.

Dede who had accompanied us produced a car which took us to the British Consulate in San Sebastian. Three days later we were taken to the British Embassy in Madrid, where one week later we were joined by the other three members of our crew, Sgts Mills, King and Naylor, who had followed the same route as Bob and myself.

From there we were taken to Gibraltar, where we were given new uniforms and interviewed. After three days we all embarked on a ship bound for Greenock. We got there safely and proceeded to London where we were debriefed by officers from MI9, one of whom was Airey Neave (ex-escaper from Germany). Later that day we had a full debriefing at Air Ministry concerning what happened on the Cologne raid, when we were able to emphasise that it was due entirely to the courage of F/O Manser that we had been able to escape from the aircraft after it had been hit.

I wrote to W/Cdr Oxley, CO of No. 50 Squadron giving him a full report of the raid, but omitted the details of our subsequent evasion. Shortly afterwards the Victoria Cross was awarded posthumously to F/O Manser. I was awarded the DFM.

It was only six weeks since I'd left Betty in a strange hotel in Lincoln and now I was back with her after the most memorable experience of my life. How lucky can you get?

After some leave I resumed flying, but this time with Coastal Command. I did a GR (General Reconnaissance) course and then I was posted to No. 461 Sunderland Squadron at RAF Hamworthy (Poole), where I joined Dudley Marrow's crew as second pilot. They were a great bunch, all Aussies except for the WOM/AG, an RAF type, Larry Donnelly, who was also ex-Bomber Command like myself and who also held the DFM.

I flew with the crew until 1943, when I went on a flying boat skippers course, after which I was posted to 201 Squadron in Northern Ireland. During my operational tour with them I was lucky enough to be awarded the DSO, DFC and Bar. When I finished my tour I went back to the OTU at Alness as an instructor. It was while I was there that I was reminded of the events of 1942.

In the summer of 1945, I received a letter from a Major in the US Army Medical Corps who turned out to be the brother of Armand Leviticus, the Dutchman who had given me the suit when we were together at Dilsen in the 'Comete' Escape Line. The major was in Belgium where he had learned that Armand had been arrested in Paris and sent to a Concentration Camp, where he had died a few weeks before the war ended. He was now trying to trace Armand's movements prior to his arrest and could I help him?

Luckily he had managed to contact Guus Uderkerken in Liege who had given him my name and who had told him I'd been with Armand prior to him going to Paris. I wrote back telling him that I'd only been with Armand at Dilsen and then Liege, where we had parted company. I was sorry I couldn't give him any further information. By this time I'd completely forgotten about the suit Armand had given me which was still in the wardrobe at my home in London. I thought that was the end of the matter, but it wasn't.

In December 1945, I was demobbed and returned to London, where I tried to settle down in civvy street, but in 1948 we decided to emigrate to New Zealand. We sold our house, got rid of all the oddments we couldn't carry by air and flew to New Zealand via Australia in 1949, where we settled down and where we have lived ever since.

We came back to Europe in the summer of 1974 for a holiday, during which time we went to Belgium where I was able to visit the farm in which we'd been given shelter in 1942. The old people had died but the younger brother and his sister now ran the farm and were delighted to see me again. During our stay we were entertained by the Town Council of Bree. While there I endeavoured to trace the young couple who had brought the bicycles to the farm and had taken us to Dilsen, but I was unable to do so. However when we went to Brussels I was able to renew acquaintance with some of the other surviving members of the 'Comete' Line who had helped us.

Our holiday ended and we returned to New Zealand. Some time later we were sent a copy of a Flemish newspaper which featured our visit to Bree. It also contained a letter from Jean Bruels, who turned out to be the young man who had brought us the bikes. I got in touch with him and during our correspondence he recalled the whole incident. He also remembered Armand Leviticus stating that he had been a Dutch diamond merchant travelling under the assumed name of von Statton. He had escaped from Amsterdam with a fortune in diamonds sewn in his clothing. Up to that time I hadn't mentioned in my letters that Armand had given me one of his suits. When I did he replied that it was almost certain that some of the diamonds were in that particular suit.

Whether that was so, we will never know, but if it is, it might explain Armand's insistent request that I return the suit to him if and when he got to England. There is no chance of confirmation because as far as I'm concerned the suit was thrown out with all the other oddments when we emigrated. It could be that there is a fortune in diamonds in some London garbage dump, or maybe that some 'Totter' got lucky!

The 'Comete' Escape Line members assisted shot-down Allied aircrew without any regard for their own safety and in doing so many among them, some of my helpers included, paid a terrible price.

Armand Leviticus, Gertrude Moors and Francoise Usandizaga died in Ravensbruk Cocentration Camp.

Henri Steinbeck's father was shot by the Gestapo when they raided his flat in Brussels. His mother was arrested and died in Ravensbruk. Henri himself made a daring escape during the raid, jumping from a window dressed only in his pyjamas. He eventually escaped to England and visited me at my home in 1943 when I was on leave. I believe he joined the Free Belgian Forces afterwards.

Giselle Evrard and both her parents were arrested, her father being imprisoned in solitary confinement in a fortress west of Berlin. He survived the war, but died shortly after his release. Giselle and her mother were sent to the Concentration Camps at Ravensbruk and Mauthausen.

Little Andree Dumont (Nadine) and her father were arrested. He was shot, she was sent to Ravensbruk. Luckily she survived.

Andree (Dede) de Jongh and her father suffered the same fate, he being shot and she being sent to Ravensbruk. Fortunately she also survived.

Charlie Morelle and his sister Elvire were both arrested and imprisoned, Charlie in the Dachau Concentration Camp, where he died a few days after the Liberation. Elvire was sent to Ravensbruk but fortunately she survived.

Our guide across the Pyrenees, Florentino, survived but was crippled when he was shot in the knee during one of his crossings.

The 'Comete' Line rescued 770 shot-down aircrew. In doing so 216 Resistance members were shot, or died in Concentration Camps. At least another 700 were arrested and held in prison until the Liberation in 1945.

Flight Lieutenant Les Baveystock DSO DFC and Bar DFM, died in 1997 after a long illness. Before he died he presented his decorations and medals to the Royal Air Force Museum at Hendon, where they are permanently displayed in the 'Wings Over Water' section. A fitting tribute to a great flier.

Larry Donnelly, Pete Jensen and Les Baveystock, Sydney 1987.

F/Lt Les Baveystock DSO DFC★ DFM.

Nine
Battling Over The Bay

At the beginning of 1943, the battle against the U-boats was hotting up in both the Atlantic and the Bay of Biscay. 461 Squadron was heavily involved carrying out patrols to search out and destroy the U-boats as they proceeded through the Bay to and from their bases in Occupied France, to the Western Atlantic, where they preyed on our convoys of merchant ships.

Over the years since the beginning of the war, improvements in submarine detection had taken place. We now had aircraft fitted with powerful searchlights (Leigh Lights) and airborne radar to seek out U-boats during day and night. As well as Sunderland and Catalina flying boats; land-based Whitleys, Wellingtons, Halifaxes and Liberators were used in the search and strike role, while Beaufighters and Mosquitoes were used to intercept the German Ju88s used to protect the U-boat in transit. To counter this, the German Admiral Dönitz ordered his submarine captains to sail on the surface during daylight (where they were faster than when submerged) instead of at night, and to remain on the surface and fight if attacked by Allied aircraft. This they did in packs for mutual protection.

This resulted in an increase of sightings and attacks by our aircraft but the Germans improved and increased the amount of anti-aircraft armament fitted to the U-boats. Their normal armament was supplemented with batteries of quadruple 20mm flak guns, so any Allied aircraft attacking a pack had to run the gauntlet of a formidable flak barrage. In addition the Germans patrolled the Bay with formations of long-range Ju88 twin-engine fighters and short-range Fw190 fighters. Consequently there were numerous attacks on U-boats and aerial combats.

During the period May to August 1943, a critical phase in the anti U-boat war, more sinkings of U-boats and more aerial combats took place in and over the Bay than at any other time or place during the Second World War. A total of twenty-eight U-boats were sunk and eighteen damaged, and twenty-six German aircraft were shot down in combat – but the price was high. Seventy-seven Allied aircraft were lost and forty-four damaged.

As well as sending out submarines from the Occupied French Ports, the Germans also sent out fast merchant ships (blockade runners) to take precision instruments to their Japanese Allies, who in return sent the Germans raw materials such as rubber and other commodities which were in short supply and urgently required by the German war industries. These ships would leave their port in France under cover of darkness and speed south through the Bay of Biscay to the South Atlantic then head east for Japan. Our Intelligence was alerted to this and when information was received that one of them was either inbound or outbound through the Bay, action was initiated to intercept and sink it.

On 10 April 1943, we took off in our Sunderland from Pembroke Dock, where we had recently set up shop to replace No. 210 Catalina Squadron who had taken our place at Hamworthy. We were scheduled to carry out an anti-submarine patrol over the Bay of Biscay. After a few hours we reached our patrol area and commenced searching, but our search was cut short when I received a W/T message (being on watch at the time) from our Group Headquarters instructing us to divert to the southern area of the Bay where a blockade runner was reported to be on its way back from Japan. I passed it to the skipper and Jock our navigator who worked out an intercept. Our task was to find the ship and home onto it a strike force of Hampden torpedo bombers which had been detailed to sink it.

Eventually we reached the area where the target had been reported and began our search. It was a fine day with about 6/10ths of patchy cloud and as we flew into a clear patch, we struck lucky and spotted the ship ahead. However, it was now being escorted by German destroyers who opened fire on us. The fire was quite heavy and we took evasive action from the flak and retired to what we hoped was a safe distance.

I sent a message to Group Headquarters informing them of the ship's position and that we were under fire from the destroyer escort. They instructed us that the Hampden force was on its way and we were to home it onto the target. We continued circling while I sent homing signals as we dodged the flak. However, shortly before the Hampdens arrived, our gunners reported that five Ju88s had arrived in the area (obviously sent out as air cover) and were coming in to attack us. We beat a hasty retreat as I sent a message to Group informing them we were under fighter attack. Actually we couldn't have stayed much longer in the area as we were now at PLE (Prudent Limit of Endurance).

We reached what we hoped was safe cloud cover when suddenly Jock who was keeping watch from the astrodome, shouted over the intercom 'Get down, get down, skipper, our bloody tail's poking out of the cloud top!' When we had reached cloud and let down into it, the skipper had then resumed level flight, thinking we were safe and unaware that the top of the tail-fin was exposed with Ju88s homing in on it fast. He quickly stuffed the nose down and we descended into thicker cloud. Fortunately for us, but not for the Hampden boys, the 88s transferred their attentions to them. We got away unscathed, but the Hampdens weren't so lucky. Listening on the W/T I heard them report they had achieved some hits, but that they were under heavy attack from both the destroyers and the German fighters and had suffered casualties.

Setting course for home we proceeded on our way, taking advantage of the cloud cover until we were well away from the area. However when we were relaxing and congratulating ourselves that we were out of trouble, just south of the Scillies we ran into a flight of Fw190s. Luckily before they saw us and got within attacking range we were again able to escape into cloud. We eventually landed safely at Pembroke Dock after being airborne for what had been nearly thirteen very eventful hours.

Years after the war, I attended a Sunderland Reunion in Melbourne, where I renewed acquaintance with the surviving members of my Australian crew. During our reminiscences, Jock our navigator recalled the incident in the Bay. He said when we were attacked by the Ju88s he had asked me if I'd informed Group of our predicament.

Apparently I'd replied that I'd bashed out the message four times before I could stop my hand shaking on the Morse Key!

In common with all operational units, every squadron's aircrew were convinced theirs was the best squadron, theirs was the best crew and theirs was the best aircraft. This especially applied to the flying-boat tradesmen aircrew, who were responsible for the day-to-day servicing and who probably spent more time on their boats than they did ashore. As well as flying and servicing the boat they had to take their turn on a 'Duty Hand' roster. This was a form of security guard comprising two tradesmen aircrew SNCOs who manned the boat when it was moored to ensure safety and security. It was a twenty-four hour duty, so it could sometimes include a twelve to thirteen hour anti-sub patrol. Usually the duty wasn't too exacting but sometimes snags could arise and I recall one such occasion in the late spring of 1943.

At the end of a thirteen hour anti-sub patrol over the Bay, we landed at Pembroke Dock in our boat 'U' for Uncle (referred to by the less couth members of the crew as 'U' for Cough!) and taxied up the Trots in Angle Bay toward the mooring buoys in the dock harbour.

On the bridge, Dudley our skipper and Jimmy Leigh (who had replaced Les Baveystock as our second pilot) were at the controls. Behind them Jock (navigator) and Pete (WOp/AG) were finishing cooking their logs, while Lance and Bubbles (flight engineers) kept a watchful eye on the engine instruments. Down in the galley Dusty (WOp/AG) and myself (WOM/AG) had the galley hatches open in preparation for launching the sea-drogues. In the bows Pierre (flight rigger), had retracted the front gun turret, fixed the small detachable ladder on the outside of the boat and looped the mooring-up strop around the aircraft bollard in the nose. Beside him Bunny (AG) was holding the boat-hook waiting to assist Pierre in the mooring-up operation, which was a team task and could be a tricky business especially at Pembroke Dock.

The mooring-up buoy hove in sight and Dudley eased the boat towards it. As it got closer he gave the signal by sounding the galley-buzzer for Dusty and myself to launch the two sea-drogues. The launching of the drogues slowed the boat's progress enabling Bunny in the bows to snare the loop on the mooring buoy with the boat-hook. As soon as he caught it he flung up his arm to signal Dudley to cut the engines. At the same time, Pierre, acrobatically hanging by his legs from the ladder on the side of the fuselage smartly threaded the strop through the loop on the buoy and wound it round the aircraft bollard. Pierre and Bunny then completed the mooring up while Dusty and I recovered the sea drogues. Lance and Bubbles prepared to receive the refuelling 'scow' and Dudley, Jimmy, Jock and Pete cleared up the bridge in preparation for going ashore.

Eventually the crew dinghy arrived and the crew members who were required for debriefing (myself included) piled on board, while the others remained to finish off the after-flight chores, Once ashore we proceeded to the 'Ops Block' where the pilots were debriefed by the 'duty spy' (Intelligence Officer) while I went to the Signals Office, handed in the 'Syko' code machine, our two carrier pigeons (nick-named Bishop and Ball after two First World War aces) and carried out a signals debrief. Our patrol had been without incident, so debriefing didn't take long and after checking our position on the Readiness Roster to ascertain when we could expect to fly our next sortie, we dispersed to our respective messes, that is all except myself. I had to return to the boat as I was Duty Hand with Pierre until the following morning. Before I left I went to the Sergeants' Mess where I refilled the two water-cans I'd brought ashore and scrounged some titbits from a sympathetic WAAF cook to supplement our rations.

By the time I'd got back to the boat, the engineers had finished refuelling and checking the engines. Bunny and Dusty had finished cleaning the guns, so they all went ashore leaving Pierre and myself to mind the store. We finished the cleaning up, then had a fry-up and, as we'd been on the go since 0400 hours that morning, we decided to have an early night. So after washing up, I called Flying Control on the R/T to tell them we were shutting up shop. They informed me that a fairly vigorous front was forecast for our area, so before climbing into our sleeping bags in the ward-room we checked the moorings. We were soon fast asleep but it wasn't for long, because for once the Seaweed and Corns merchants (Met Forecasters) were correct and the vigorous front arrived as forecast.

At Pembroke Dock there is a rise and fall of tide of twenty-two feet between tides and if they are running in gale conditions, it can cause problems, especially if the tide, as in our case, was on the beam. Consequently, the boat was weather-cocking and pitching into wind and the tide on the beam was causing a rolling action. We had a real 'mal de mer' situation, but fatigue is a good anaesthetic and we slept on.

It must have been about midnight when the boat bucked quite viciously and I awoke with a start. I lay there trying to gather my fuddled sleep-ridden wits and then I heard it, the unmistakeable sound of water splashing. Grabbing my hand-torch, I switched it on to shine towards the bows where the noise seemed come from. In the light I could see water running along the deck, so I hastily left my sleeping-bag yelling to Pierre as I did so, 'Holy cow, we're awash sport!' (By this time I could speak 'Strine' like a native!)

Pierre came to and we dressed as quickly as we could. Switching on the ward-room lights we made our way forward. The boat was pitching and rolling and as we got near the bows, we could see that the front turret wasn't wound fully forward and every time the boat pitched, water was being scooped up into the aircraft to run along the decks into the bilges. We hastily checked the moorings and after ensuring they were secure, also wound the turret fully forward double-checking to make sure there was no further ingress of water.

Our next task was to ascertain how much water had been shipped into the bilges, so we went to the bomb-room and opened up an inspection hatch. The light from our torches revealed a considerable amount swirling around in the hull. Pierre said, 'Come on sport, we'd better get cracking and get rid of this smartly, because if anything happens to his beloved boat, Dudley will have our pelts for pull-through, thank gawd for the APU.' He was referring to the auxiliary power unit, comprising a small petrol-driven engine housed in the rear of the starboard inner-engine nacelle, which could be used to drive a bilge-pump or an electrical generator to charge the batteries.

We climbed up the ladder from the galley to the bridge, opened up the top hatch and clambered out onto the starboard wing. In normal conditions you had to watch your step even in daylight, but in the dark with the rain pelting and the boat rolling and pitching it was really dicey. However we managed and got cracking. While I held the torch Pierre undid the catches, releasing part of the leading-edge section of the starboard wing near the inner engine and lowered it to use as a working platform.

I stood on it, opened up the engine nacelle, primed the APU and, as luck would have it, managed to start it at the first attempt. Pierre then took over and when it was running smoothly, he switched on the bilge-pump, but to our utter dismay, it failed to work. After several fruitless attempts it was evident there was only one alternative – muscle power – we would have to pump the water from the bilges by hand. It is at times such as this that Australians manage to express bitter frustration in their own inimitable way. Pierre looked at me and said, 'Wouldn't it bite yer flamin' bum!'

We shut down the APU, secured the wing leading-edge and made our way to the bomb-room, where we laboriously rigged the hand-pump, opened up the bomb-doors, slung out the pipe-attachment and got cracking. It took some time and considerable effort before we managed to get all the surplus water from the bilges and by the time we'd finished we were physically shattered. Pierre echoed both our sentiments when he said, 'Cobber, I'm worn down to me flamin' cap badge!' We staggered back to the ward-room where we collapsed on the bunks, to sleep soundly till wakened by the relief Duty Hands clattering on board. A couple of hours later, Dudley and the rest of the crew arrived. Dudley said to Pierre and I, 'That was quite a storm last night, you two must have had a rough time.' I winked at Pierre and replied, 'Skipper, you don't know the half of it.'

As it turned out it was fortunate that nothing untoward did happen to 'U' for Cough that night, otherwise it may not have pulled off one of the most amazing coincidences of the Second World War.

On 30 July 1943, aircraft 'U' for Uncle of No. 461 Squadron, Royal Australian Air Force, sank submarine *U-461* of the German Navy in the Bay of Biscay! The incident has been described as one of the most epic battles between submarine and aircraft to take place during the Second World War.

In the book *Flying Porcupines*, a biography of Flt Lt Dudley Marrows DSO DFC, written by Maureen Lakey, Dudley describes the action:

We were diverted from a normal anti-submarine patrol by Group to a position where a U-boat had been sighted. The first position they gave us proved to be false, so we commenced a search pattern. Another position was received from Group, so we set off again. As we neared the estimated position, the wireless operator reported increased traffic from naval vessels and other aircraft in the area. P/O Jimmy Leigh who was scanning the horizon with binoculars, excitedly reported that there was not one submarine, but three. They were sailing steadily on the surface in a tight formation. Initially I thought they were destroyers because of their size and wash. I was to learn later that two of the U-boats, U-461 and another were large refuellers known as 'milch cow' refueller submarines and their loss would be a serious blow to the German Navy.

As we flew towards them I developed a plan of attack which paid off. The U-boats had attracted RAF Coastal Command Liberators, two Halifaxes, a Catalina and a US Air Force Liberator. It was quite an air circus and there were also five RN anti-submarine sloops some distance away homing in on the subs. Flying above at high altitude observing the scene was a sole Luftwaffe Ju88. By the time we reached an attack position, the Liberator and the Catalina were diving on the U-boats making feint attacks, From height the Halifaxes were dropping 600lb bombs resulting in near misses but which had little effect. To combat the air attacks the U-boats were manoeuvring in formation, keeping their bows toward the attacking aircraft maximising their fire power and putting up a formidable barrage.

I had now decided on my attack routine, I would try to avoid the U-boats' maximum fire by going in at sea level hoping to catch the U-boats when they were broadside to the swell making them an unsteady gun platform. Also I hoped we would be shielded from the two inner subs who wouldn't be able to depress their guns to hit us as I attacked the outer one.

I carried out one feint attack but the fire power from the U-boats was so intense that the shrapnel pummelled the fuselage of the Sunderland like a shower of hail, so I decided to go in as low as possible.

I flew into the attack, violently zig-zagging as we lost height to sea level. We initially copped the full impact of about twenty-seven heavy calibre cannon and heavy machine-guns from each U-boat involved, some eighty-one cannon and machine-guns in all. Our front and mid-upper gunners returned accurate machine-gun fire which I believe made the difference between us being shot down into the sea and being here today to tell the story.

At this stage I was concentrating on my alignment and distance to drop the depth-charges – we had no sights in those days, it all depended on the pilot's judgement. I could see the German gunners throwing themselves about the submarines to avoid our gunners' fire. Some U-boat seamen were slumped around their guns obviously hit, while others shook their fists at us. A Royal Navy report of the action which I later received claimed that my gunners had shot one of the gunners on U-461 through the middle of his forehead.

My plan was to straddle the submarine with a stick of depth-charges. The Sunderland carried eight, I would drop seven and keep one in reserve. I flew as low as possible, just skimming the wave tops. Nearing the submarine, I had to fly straight and level waiting for the submarine to go out of view below the nose of the Sunderland – a most critical time. Then, as practised many times, I had to count ten then press the depth-charge release button. I had to pull up violently after I'd dropped my depth-charges to avoid hitting the submarine's conning tower. My low approach paid off, because as I'd hoped the two outer U-boats couldn't depress their guns low enough to fire at me until we had passed over 'our' U-boat.

As soon as we passed over the conning tower I dropped to sea level and did a steep turn to port to avoid the fire from the other U-boats. Our gunners kept up their fire as we flew away. I had no idea how accurate my attack had been until my navigator Jock Rolland called out over the intercom, 'You've got one.' He was still hanging out of the hatch photographing the results of the attack despite the violent evasive action I was taking to avoid the U-boat gunfire.

When I was able to return to the attack scene the other two U-boats had moved away. There was a large oil slick over the spot where U-461 had sunk. Debris, survivors and dead bodies could be seen in the water. The survivors had nothing but their life-jackets. I recall that it was not a pleasant sensation seeing the Germans in the sea so obviously distressed, so I made another run over them and dropped a dinghy, which fell accurately among them and inflated. I could see the survivors clambering into the dinghy and was about to make a low run to attack on the two remaining submarines when I saw water *spouts around them – gunfire from the RN sloops. As I wasn't certain we had sufficient fuel to get back to base, we signalled the sloops there were survivors in the water and set course for home.*

Half an hour later there was more action when the crew spotted another U-boat on the surface. Although we were low on fuel I attacked immediately. I had one depth-charge left but as I was setting up the depth-charge release apparatus, I accidentally switched on the auto pilot, so when I went to level out from my attack, I couldn't bring the Sunderland out of the dive. With the help of Jimmy, my co-pilot, we wrestled the Sunderland back to level flight. The U-boat had elected to remain on the surface and fight and its anti-aircraft fire hit the main spar in the port main-plane damaging the depth-charge carriage, so now we couldn't drop the charge. Our gunners continued strafing the U-boat as other crew members struggled to extinguish a fire caused by the U-boat's machine-gun fire. The U-boat then submerged and being aware that this latest attack had taxed our fuel supply I decided to return to base. However the flight engineer's fuel readings and the navigator's calculations gave warning we'd be lucky to get as far as the Scilly Isles. With only 19 gallons of fuel left the Sunderland landed at the Scillies where we laboriously refuelled the aircraft from four-gallon cans transferred by hand from a naval whaler.

Dudley and Jock Rolland made reports to Coastal Command Headquarters about the attack on four U-boats resulting in one kill. But any feelings they had of a job well done were cut short when their superiors gave Dudley a reprimand for dropping a dinghy to the U-boat survivors! They made the point that he risked his own and his crews' lives by depriving them of a dinghy which might have been needed. However, for his achievement in sinking *U-461*, Dudley was awarded the Distinguished Flying Cross.

After the war, Pete Jensen WOp/AG, with the assistance of other interested Sunderland survivors formed a committee who organised a tour of the south of England and Wales from where they had operated. It was a success, so they had the idea of contacting their old enemies of the war years.

Through letters contact was established with the German ex-service organisations and visits were arranged. During the first, which took place in 1979, the highlight of the trip was to the U-Boat memorial at Kiel. Wherever they went they were feted and entertained.

During another visit in 1983, Pete Jensen obtained further information concerning the survivors of *U-461*, eleven of them including Captain Wolf Steibler. The outcome was that in 1986, Pete and his ex-461 Squadron party met Wolf Steibler in Munich who made them most welcome escorting and entertaining them throughout their visit.

Two years later they met again but this time it was in Australia when Wolf came as one of the elite 'Cape Horn' sailors, attending the Australia Day Bicentennial celebrations in 1988. During his stay he was fittingly entertained by Dudley and Pete's families and he and his one-time enemies became firm friends. During his visit Captain Wolf Steibler gave them his version of the events of the battle they fought in the Bay of Biscay on 30 July 1943.

U-boats *U-461*, *U-462* and *U-507* left Lorient on the evening of 29 July 1943 with

Captain Wolf Steibler as senior officer in charge of the group:

> *I ordered that they cruise on the surface all night and rendezvous at a point in the Bay of Biscay next morning. U-461 and U-507 made the rendezvous but U-462 was missing. We stayed on the surface as long as we dared and I was about to give the order to submerge when there were flashes of light, it was U-462 signalling with his searchlight.*
>
> *We sailed back to discover that he had been submerged all night and had flat batteries (using his searchlight had flattened them further), so it was impossible for him to submerge. I had to make a decision, I knew that to remain on the surface during the day was dangerous, so should I stay with U-462 and protect it or submerge and leave it to its fate? I decided to remain surfaced, but soon we were spotted and the battle began.*

The depth-charge from the Sunderland broke *U-461* in two; something caught on Wolf's clothing and he was dragged down to a considerable depth before he was released and came to the surface.

During the battle they had seen a Halifax bomb *U-462* and assumed it had been hit when they saw the crew abandon it, apparently this was not so, the bomb had missed and the crew had scuttled the boat. They all had one-man dinghies. Wolf and his survivors only had life-preservers and swam to the dinghy dropped from the Sunderland. They put the wounded men into it and the rest stayed in the water holding on to the edge of the dinghy.

The sloops then arrived and began depth-charging *U-507* as it submerged. They were only about 800 to 1,000 metres from the *U-461* survivors. Wolf said the men in the water suffered excruciating pain. They pulled themselves out of the water as far as they could but Wolf said his stomach was forced into his chest and his eyeballs felt as if they were being forced out of his head. He honestly thought he was dying. He was very bitter about the whole affair, as he put it, 'I sacrificed two good boats and two good crews to save a boat which scuttled itself.' The third boat, *U-507*, was sunk by the sloops.[1]

Six weeks after sinking *U-461*, Dudley and his crew were again on patrol over the Bay. They had a new aircraft and three new crew members. Jock Rolland had finished his tour as navigator and had been replaced by George Done. Bob Webster, WOp/AG, had replaced me, as I had been posted to commence pilot training. One of my many applications had finally borne fruit, due mainly to the recommendations from my Aussie sponsors. As it turned out my posting was timely! The third new member was Sgt Eshleberry, who had taken over as flight engineer. This was his first operational sortie with the crew, a debut I'm sure he will remember! Dudley takes over the story:

> *We were well out over the Bay when a voice came over the intercom, 'Skipper there's five aircraft to the east heading our way – no, there's six.' I knew they must be German and instructed the wireless operator to send a signal back to base, 'enemy aircraft attack imminent' and giving our position.*
>
> *Our altitude was 2,000 feet. I immediately turned west to take the Germans further away from their base and thus reduce their time available to attack. There was a slight amount of*

Captain Wolf Steibler.

F/Lt Dudley Marrows.

cloud to the west, so I didn't let down to sea level (where they couldn't attack us from below) but made for the cloud, jettisoning our depth-charges on the way. We had ample time to get ready. All gun positions were manned, including the two extra galley guns and the VGO which could be fired by the second pilot.

It was confirmed that our attackers were Ju88 long-range fighters. When they caught up with us, they split into two formations of three, one formation on each side of us. We had a good side-on view of them. One who we deduced was the leader stood off and began controlling systematic attacks. His tactics were well planned and different to those we'd run across during our training in aerial combat. First one would turn into attack and as soon as we began our evasive tactic, another attacked us from the other side. This was repeated time after time.

Our navigator, George Done was acting as our fire controller, timing his orders to me to turn, from his position in the astrodome (a plastic bubble aft of the cockpit on the upper fuselage), from where he had an almost unobstructed view for 360 degrees around and above the aircraft, but not below it, where the aircraft fuselage and wings obstructed his view.

George passed his instructions to me over the intercom, 'aircraft to starboard closing in, lining up for attack, turn starboard now.' I would veer hard right in a diving turn more or less directly at the attacking aircraft. The view then was of the Ju88 heading straight at us guns blazing until it broke off the attack – either concerned with the possibility of collision, or by the fire from our guns. We could actually see the head and shoulders of the pilot and other crew members.

While this was going on I would hear, 'Aircraft to port, attacking, turn now.' I would still be in the turn to starboard and all I could do was to pick up speed by diving and moving in a left turn in an attempt to make it difficult for him to have a steady target and for our mid-upper and tail-turrets to get a better shot.

What a target the enemy had, the Sunderland then being broadside on. Our main armament, our four-gun tail turret, was almost immediately put out of action when its hydraulic lines were severed during the first side-on attack. After attacking, the Ju88s would resume formation while the second pair came at us using the same tactics. This was repeated several times. Then one of the mid-upper guns jammed, so we had only one gun left in the mid-upper, two single galley guns, a damaged nose turret and Jimmy Leigh's 'special' from the second pilot position.

In between attacks, Jimmy and I were endeavouring to assess the damage, mainly to the engines. The indications were loss of power, the instruments going haywire and smoke coming from the damaged engines. The net result of the enemy's tactics was that our large vulnerable side was presented to each attacking Ju88 and our depleted fire-power was split. The summation of our combat report, when we eventually got back, stands out in my memory. 'Much can be learned from this combat.' I wonder whether they learned anything that could be effectively applied. I doubt it! We had superiority over single Ju88 attacks and packs when they attacked one at a time, but not against this well-planned and well-executed tactic.

During this combat there was no move to attack from underneath, so I utilised our height to do steeper diving turns. Throughout, we were being hit. A canon shell exploded in the front turret, knocking the gun off its mounting, also wounding the gunner Pierre Bamber with shrapnel, but he continued to use the gun, hand held. On one occasion I looked briefly round to see the wireless operator Bob Webster at his desk with blood streaming from his face. A 20mm canon shell had exploded in the wireless set cutting his face with shrapnel – not badly, as it turned out. All this time Jimmy Leigh was blazing away from the second pilot position, with his .303 VGO, loaded with incendiaries. I could see a trail of flame going away.

I was losing power. The instruments showed that first one, then two, then three engines had been hit. I was having real trouble maintaining height and manoeuvring and as I lost height I realised we would have to ditch, so I advised the crew. However, at sea level I found a little more power and told the crew, 'We're not done yet,' but after suffering more damage, I couldn't maintain height and gave the ditching signal.

The crew took up their ditching positions to withstand the impact, while I made the decision as to how I would ditch – along the swells and across wind. I was lucky and able to make a virtually power-off landing, the only damage being to the struts of one float which were broken. We settled in the water almost normally, but with one wing down.

All this time we were being fired on. That Sunderland was a tough old bird! On landing, emergency evacuation procedures were carried out as we'd done so many times in training. Up on the wing, in a sequence position, individual crew took with them, dinghies, flame floats, a Verey pistol and cartridges, emergency radio, pigeons and food. Everything went as planned except that we weren't able to retrieve the dinghy stowed in the back of the aircraft.

Being skipper, in true naval tradition, I was last to leave the aircraft and get up on the wing. I am even now left with three vivid impressions – a line of machine-gun hits across the starboard main-plane as the 88s carried out their last attack; the look of 'what's next' on the faces of the crew; and the enemy aircraft waggling their wings in salute as they flew away.

They were probably short of fuel. They had a clear opportunity to blast hell out of us, but didn't. I firmly believe that this was, in its way, a repayment for our dropping a dinghy to the survivors of U-461, saving fifteen of its crew. One of the Ju88s must have taken a photo of us, because sometime later a picture of us on the wing of the ditched Sunderland appeared in a 'captured' German magazine.

Well, there we were on the wing, in the middle of the Bay of Biscay, on an aircraft that was still floating, albeit one wing down, in a heavy swell. We had time to salvage more gear, so I went back into the aircraft and handed up every bit of food that was left and a few other odd things. I couldn't pass the remaining dinghy, because the aircraft was pitching, lurching wildly and I had no idea how long I had to get out. The Sunderland was slowly sinking, water was spouting through the canon shell holes. I managed to grab the dinghy and pop it over the side.

Back on the wing with a bit more time to look around. Pierre was in trouble with his wounds but didn't make a fuss. Bob Webster with his facial cuts – no problem. Bunny Sydney had been scalded with a kettle of boiling water which had been left on the stove when we were attacked. I was the only other one wounded with a shrapnel cut on my little finger – what luck!

I had real decisions to make. The dinghy I had dropped over the side was gradually drifting away. There were jagged edges around the canon and machine-gun holes in the fuselage which were a hazard to the rubber dinghies, so believing the aircraft would sink, I decided we should board the dinghies. Jimmy Leigh volunteered to swim out to the one already in the water which needed to be inflated. We inflated the other two dinghies on the wing, loaded them up and dropped them into the water. The wing was still some eight feet above the water line so it was necessary for us to jump into the water and swim to and clamber into the dinghies. Pierre was worried, in addition to his injuries he couldn't swim. I told him not to worry I would get him to the dinghy. He promptly jumped in the water. I followed and got him to the nearest dinghy.

To get into a dinghy during practice sessions in calm water, was relatively easy for a fit man. Out there in rough water, with tired men, it was a hell of a lot harder. Pierre remained in the water until all the others got in, then together we got him in – he didn't make a whimper.

Then our troubles began. At first there were five in each of the larger dinghies and Jimmy Leigh on his own in the smaller one. One of the larger ones split along a shrapnel cut so badly that we had no hope of plugging the damage, so those five had to get out and join the other five in the other large dinghy with as much gear as they could manage.

Ten men in a dinghy built to hold six! Then to add to our worries the smaller dinghy split. I'll never forget the look on Jimmy Leigh's face when he swam over to us. He hung onto the side of our dinghy and I could see that he was thinking it wouldn't be possible for him to fit in, and the dinghy remain with freeboard, but we managed to get him in.

Bunny Sydney, an ex-surf lifesaver, rigged up a flap which was attached to the outside of the dinghy ring, providing a splash shield about 18 inches high, I sat enough of the crew on the dinghy ring to hold up the splash flap with their backs. We now had 11 men in a six-man dinghy. On settling down I made a close examination for other cuts or leaks and made sure that none of our other possessions might cut the dinghy fabric – we even thought about pulling the metal buttons off our trousers!

After making an assessment of provisions and equipment we found that the pigeons carefully brought across from the split dinghy in their cage, had drowned. There was some discussion as to whether we should keep them to eat, but by this time most of us were feeling a bit squeamish, so overboard went the pigeons. Unfortunately most of our rations and other equipment had been lost. We had a Verey pistol but no cartridges, so over it went. The dinghy radio had also gone, so the only thing we had left was one flame float.

We then suffered violent sea-sickness and we were in for a long night. We did what we could to keep our spirits up and kept up the splash flap to shield our backs. Without it the dinghy would have been flooded. As the aircraft radio had been rendered useless by a 20mm canon shell we hadn't been able to get out an accurate position report, but we got a lucky break.

In the dark of the night we heard an aircraft coming directly towards us and all of a sudden we were engulfed in white light. It was a RAF Catalina equipped with a Leigh Light (searchlight), who had homed onto us using radar, thinking we were a submarine. The Catalina stayed with us for a while, sending the appropriate signals back to base. Before they left they signalled by Aldis lamp that a Liberator was on its way.

When dawn came we saw the Liberator searching some way off. We used our prized, protected flame float, which in addition to flame (for night-time) gives off a plume of smoke. The Liberator came towards us and signalled that help was on the way. Not long afterwards we had another stroke of luck, we saw smoke on the horizon. It was from the famous Captain Walker's flotilla of anti submarine sloops – they had been at the southern end of their sweep and were on their way home when they got the signal to pick us up. We ran a lottery to see if we could estimate the time at which we would be picked up.

They were indeed a welcome sight. Captain Walker's command sloop came alongside and dropped a net over the side. Another never-to-be forgotten memory – stiff, wet and cold, still somewhat seasick, climbing that rope net. With the ship rolling and dipping it was quite an adventure. The ship's crew helped Pierre and one or two others up the net.

Once on board the crew couldn't do enough for us. Captain Walker arranged for the other sloops in the flotilla to come closer to the Command sloop and using a loud-hailer he informed them all that we were the crew of the Sunderland which had sunk U-461, in the air-submarine battle in which they had played a major part. A rousing cheer went up.

After we had been given dry clothes, hot cocoa and hot baths, Captain Walker questioned why we had left the aircraft because he had found it floating submerged with water splashing over its wings. It must have been held up by the nearly empty fuel tanks. I expressed surprise and told him I was certain it would sink and as I was worried about the dinghies being cut on the many jagged edges, I deemed it wiser to get clear of it. I often wonder if we would have fared better by staying, but on the other hand the extra weight of eleven men could have proved a problem, who knows? Captain Walker had sunk it with a depth-charge before coming to find us.

We had an interesting trip back home as passenger/guests. Captain Walker, to dispose of deteriorating depth-charges arranged an awesome demonstration for us. He made a full flotilla depth-charge attack on an imaginary submarine. An instantaneously fired pattern by all the sloops. The concussion and the large mountain of water that erupted was very impressive. I can but remember with horror, the effects those crew members of U-461 must have felt when depth-charges were being dropped around the dinghy we had dropped them. Some of them were in the dinghy and some were hanging on the outside of it. Years later, Captain Wolf Steibler told me that it felt as though their lower parts in the water were being pulverised.

On approaching the UK (Wales in fact) Captain Walker was kind enough to transfer us to another sloop which would deliver us home to Pembroke Dock. That is, all except Pierre Bamber who was taken straight to hospital in Liverpool. He was kept in for some time because there was some indecision whether they should operate to remove the shrapnel in his bladder. After intense pain he passed the piece of shrapnel with a delightful 'ping' into a pot, to the accompanying cheers from watching nurses!

When we arrived at Pembroke Dock we were met by our Commanding Officer, Wing Commander Des Douglas, who informed us that a Sunderland crew from another squadron had witnessed our battle. Also that other crews from our squadron had volunteered to go out and find us, including our ex-navigator Jock Rolland, who enhanced my reputation for determination by stating that I'd swim home if I had to!

The air battle is one of the events in my life which frequently comes to the fore in my memories. Perhaps it is because we were the losers; could I have done better, should I have descended to sea level earlier and utilised my low-flying ability? I also wonder whether Air Command, when they made a study of the tactics used by the Ju88s that day, came up with any suggestion of a better way of dealing with such attacks.

Dudley was awarded the Distinguished Service Order and the Distinguished Flying Cross, as a result of the sinking of *U-461* and the air battle with the six Ju88s which shot them down.

Alan (Bubbles) Pearce and Frank (Pierre) Bamber were each awarded the Distinguished Flying Medal.

They were a wonderful crew and it was my privilege to have known and flown with them. In May 1943, the whole crew had paid me the compliment and token of their friendship by supporting me at my wedding. Pierre was my best man.

Notes
1 Captain Wolf Steibler died in 1991, aged eighty-four.

Ten

U/T Driver Airframe (Pilot)

I left my Australian cobbers of No. 461 RAAF squadron at the beginning of August 1943, to remuster as pilot. At long last I was at the first real stage of achieving my ambition to be a pilot.

At ACRC (the Aircrew Reception Centre), Regents Park, London, my reception was, to say the least, a little daunting. I was informed that although I held Warrant Officer rank, I was now a cadet and that I would have to remove my badges of rank and wear a white (cadet) flash in my forage cap. I would however retain my Warrant Officer rate of pay and be allowed to continue wearing my Air Gunner brevet and medal ribbons.

I willingly accepted this requirement, but I discovered it could have its drawbacks. During off-duty periods wandering around London wearing a brevet and gong ribbon with no visible sign of rank, was a challenge few of the ultra zealous RAF Police patrols could resist and from time to time I was stopped by them to prove my bona fide identity. However, I must admit that their grudging apologies when they discovered I wasn't masquerading, compensated for the inconvenience, especially if I happened to be escorting a member of the fair sex!

My stay at ACRC, during which I successfully negotiated various medical and aptitude tests was quite short and I was soon on my way as a member of an intake to an ITW (Initial Training Wing) at the Yorkshire seaside resort of Scarborough.

There, our initial training comprised lectures on all the associated flying subjects e.g. Airmanship, Principles of Flight, Aero-engines, Airframes Navigation, Meteorology, Radio, Morse, Armaments and, for the benefit of the cadets straight from civvy street, a generous helping of Drill and Physical training. For this latter, SNCO cadets like myself generally found ourselves conducting the proceedings. These drill sessions took place on the sea-front where they provided a little light relief for the amused Scarborough citizens and the few fortunate holidaymakers.

At this stage of the war, cadets after completing their initial training were then sent to Flying Training (Grading) Schools where they were given flying instruction on Tiger Moths to assess their suitability to continue training as pilots. If they made the grade, they continued in the pilot training scheme, otherwise they were re-graded to be trained as either navigators, or bomb-aimers.

Following the completion of my Initial Training, I was sent to an FTS (Flying Training School) on the East Yorkshire coast to be graded. During my previous flying on Bomber and Coastal Command squadrons I had always taken every opportunity of getting my sticky fingers on the pole. However, initially I found handling the Tiger a different proposition to flying the 'heavies' and I suppose I was inclined to be slightly ham-fisted. However, heeding the advice of my ancient instructor, 'handle the stick like a debutante holding a navvy's "wotsit", not like said navvy wielding a spade!' I was able to get things sorted out and meet his approval. Some adverse weather didn't help and with flights being scrubbed, it was a little difficult to pick up from where you'd left off. Despite this I steadily got through the required exercises, take-offs, climbing, descending, straight and level, gliding, stalling, spinning and 'circuits and bumps' (take-offs and landings). My previous flying opportunities must have stood me in good stead and my progress must have been satisfactory. One murky morning after carrying out some circuits and bumps, when we taxied back to the parking 'apron', my instructor got out and yelled to me, 'Right, off you go, do a circuit, don't break your neck and bring the aircraft back in one piece'.

The adrenalin was in full flow as I taxied out to the take-off point. Arriving there I halted the aircraft across wind, did my pre-take-off check (twice!) and after making sure there were no other aircraft approaching to land I turned the Tiger into wind, lined it up and opened the throttle progressively. The tail came up and I suppose I did everything right because before I knew it the little beauty was off the ground. I climbed straight ahead endeavouring to remember my instructor's exhortations, 'Watch your airspeed, altitude, turn and slip and look out for other aircraft.' Turning across wind I continued around the circuit downwind and then managed to line up for my landing. I can't recall much about the actual touch-down, but know I achieved it without breaking the aircraft, and I was told by my instructor later that while it wasn't the best landing he'd seen, at least I'd got it down in one piece! I'd made it, passed the pilot grading requirement and I couldn't wait to commence my pilot training proper.

It was now near the end of 1943. After Grading School, I was sent to the PDC (Personnel Dispatch Centre) at Heaton Park, near Manchester to await posting to a flying school in either Canada or South Africa, When I got there I found there was quite a backlog. The Commonwealth Air Training Scheme was well established and a constant stream of would-be aviators progressed through Heaton Park. There were literally hundreds of cadets now waiting to go overseas. Because of the limited accommodation at Heaton Park, cadets were billeted out with civilian families in the vicinity. Each day we were transported to and from the PDC, where the daily regime could be described as organised chaos. The permanent staff had the unenviable task of attempting to keep the hundreds of cadets occupied and out of mischief. They did this using lectures and instructional films. Among the films shown was the well-known American Services VD film in glorious technicolour, which had the effect of making the more squeamish cadets lose their breakfasts and possibly deterred them from indulging in sex for a short time!

In December 1943, passages overseas slowed down further, so in order to relieve the build up of cadets at Heaton Park, detachments of them were sent to various operational RAF stations. I was put in charge of fifty U/T aircrew and sent to RAF Snaith, in Yorkshire, a heavy bomber station. As luck would have it, Snaith was in 4 Group, with whom I'd flown from 1939 to 1942 on my bomber tours. Also the Station Commander, Gp Capt T. Sawyer DFC turned out to have been a Flight Commander on of one of my previous squadrons when I was nearing the end of my first bomber tour. His Station

Warrant Officer, W.O. Browning, was also a well-known character in the Group pre-war. I was back in the fold!

My party of cadets was put under the jurisdiction of Warrant Officer Browning who was only too pleased to supplement his ACH/GDs (Aircraft Hands General Duties) with my willing volunteers, to carry out some of the less glamorous tasks on the station.

We were billeted in Nissen huts dispersed around the aerodrome. Inadequate heating was provided by two pot-bellied stoves, around which we huddled at night in an attempt to defeat the freezing cold. Bedclothes were supplemented with greatcoats and with other spare items of uniform draped on top. Fuel was in short supply, so it was SOP (Standard Operating Procedure) to unofficially supplement our ration from the adjacent coal compound at every opportunity. This state of inadequate heating prevailed throughout the camp as all the accommodation consisted entirely of Nissen huts, even Station Headquarters. The aforementioned Station Warrant Officer had the responsibility of ensuring that the stove in the Station Commander's office was lit and well alight before the CO arrived every morning. One morning however, things went awry – either the coal/coke was damp or the wind was in the wrong direction. When the CO opened the door to his office he was engulfed in smoke. His irate reaction was to summon his Station Warrant Officer and accuse him of attempting to turn him into a 'bloody haddock!'

This was the time in 1943 when the Bomber Command offensive was gaining momentum – the Battle of Berlin being uppermost – and the resident Halifax squadron at Snaith was heavily engaged on every possible occasion. Night after night the roar of engines shattered the silence as the aircraft took off and climbed away from the airfield to bomb Germany. Sadly after every raid the casualties were counted and I think that this and the primitive living conditions, gave my 'charges' an new insight and shattered any illusions they may have had that operational flying was all glamour and glory.

After about five weeks our attachment ended and we returned to Heaton Park to await our overseas posting. At the beginning of 1944 the backlog cleared bringing our waiting to an end, One memorable morning we were mustered and I found I was on a draft to proceed to Canada. After the usual preliminaries (a cursory medical to ensure we weren't suffering from any infectious or social diseases and the tedious task of 'clearing' from the station) we left Manchester in high spirits by train and travelled to the port of Greenock on the Clyde.

It didn't take long to get there and on arrival we embarked on our troopship, which we discovered was the French 43,000 ton ocean-going liner, the *Ille de France*. Like the *Queen Mary, Queen Elizabeth* and other large liners it had been commandeered and converted to use as a troopship. These ocean greyhounds were capable of very high speeds and were able to dash across the oceans unescorted with a minimum risk of being caught up or intercepted by U-boats.

The 'draft' for this crossing of the Atlantic comprised our RAF contingent of approximately 200 aircrew cadets en route to Canada for training and some 400 or 500 American personnel, including some aircrew who had fortunately survived an operational tour and were returning to the USA. Also there were some less heroic members of the American forces, guilty of serious misdemeanours and heading back to serve their sentences in American jails. All the innocent members of the draft were accommodated in cabins on the upper decks, while the jail-birds were incarcerated in the brig (cells in the bowels of the ship).

By the time all our accommodation had been allocated and we'd been fed, it was late in the day so, as our American comrades put it, we hit the sack. When we woke the following morning, we were under way and heading west to where the land, according to the poet, 'is bright'.

Going to the dining room (mess deck) we were agreeably surprised by the standard of the fare, which included items we, in wartime rationed Britain, hadn't seen for some time – such as white bread and butter. Some of our fellow voyagers however, were unable to appreciate this bounty, being susceptible to, and feeling the effects of the rolling main!

After breakfast we were mustered on the upper deck for instruction in lifeboat drill, something which was to be a regular occurrence throughout the voyage. On completion of the drill, we were informed by our OC (Officer Commanding) troops that we were responsible for keeping our accommodation (which would be inspected daily by the ship's officers) clean and tidy. This included all the toilet facilities, so we organised from our RAF contingent fatigue teams of LAC cadets, supervised by SNCOs. This character building task wasn't onerous and left plenty of time for other diversions such as PT (Physical Training) and the odd lecture. We were left to our own devices for the remainder of the time.

It was discovered that one of the RAF cadets was a county-class chess champion, so as a welcome change from the never-ending card games, we prevailed upon him to volunteer to instruct those who showed interest. Most of the SNCO cadets, including myself, were bitten by the bug and by the end of the voyage were keen enthusiasts. The Royal Canadian Air Force subsequently benefited from this intellectual pursuit, because later during our training at various RCAF stations, we made sure that chess sets became one of the items available in the games-rooms of their Sergeants' Messes.

Our voyage progressed without incident and as the *Ille de France* was big enough to cope with the winter weather and the Atlantic swells, most of us soon got our sea legs. As we were unescorted, our course was obviously planned to keep us well away from the normal convoy routes to lessen the risk of interception by lurking U-boats. After six days of zig-zagging we calculated we might be getting near our destination and this was confirmed unofficially by one of the ship's officers, who dropped the hint that we were on the home straight and might reach New York the following day.

Having been indoctrinated by American films and literature that a first sight of the city was not to be missed, I made sure I was up near the sharp end as we approached. It was as described – the silhouettes of the sky-scrapers were a magnificent, never to be forgotten sight. Tugs came out and guided us to our berth, where we prepared to disembark.

The USAF contingent had priority and as they left the ship a military band on the dock-side gave them a rousing and well-deserved home-coming welcome. When they had disembarked, it was our turn, so we left the ship and made our way along the docks to board a waiting train which would take us on our journey north to Canada. While we waited to depart, ladies of the American equivalent to our Women's Voluntary Service, supplied us with coffee, dough-nuts and fresh fruit.

It wasn't long before we were on our way north to our destination, the RCAF Reception and Dispatch Centre, at Monkton, New Brunswick. Our journey didn't take too long, but after the enthusiastic welcome to New York, our arrival was a bit of an anti-climax – it was discovered that one of our contingent was afflicted with mumps and this resulted in us all being placed in quarantine, incarcerated in our quarters for the next fourteen days!

When we were released, four other Warrant Officer cadets and myself went to the town of Monkton, where we celebrated at a restaurant on goodies we'd been deprived of for years – T-bone steaks and then real ice-cream!

A few days after being released from quarantine, we were informed we were to proceed to our elementary Flying Schools. Ours was at Assinaboia in Saskatchewan. It wasn't until we boarded the train and checked the location of Assiniboia on a map, that we realised we would have to travel across Canada from the north-east coast to the south-west corner, bordering America. So began one of the longest and most interesting train journeys I've ever experienced.

Our route took us via Quebec, then north of the Great Lakes and west to Winnipeg, Weyburn, Regina and finally to Assiniboia. The journey took us six days in Pullman coaches which had sleeping and dining facilities. We travelled by day at the end of which our Pullman coaches were uncoupled and shunted into a siding where we slept the night. The following morning, the carriages would be hitched up again and off we'd go. It was early spring, the scenery was eye-catching and it was quite an experience to see places which up to now had been just names on a map or in books. On the sixth day our journey ended when we reached our destination. We disembarked and boarded transport which took us to RCAF Assiniboia. Let's get airborne!

A Tiger Moth.

Eleven
Flying Training

It didn't take us long to settle in at RCAF Assiniboia. SNCO cadets like myself were accommodated in the Sergeants' Mess, where we were made most welcome by the permanent staff.

The day following our arrival we were welcomed by the Chief Instructor (a RCAF Wing Commander), who outlined the course procedure. He informed us that our flying training would take place on Fairchild Cornells, which were low-wing monoplanes, two-seat primary trainers powered by a 200hp, air-cooled 7-cylinder Ranger engine. He mentioned that they were possibly a little faster (maximum speed of 126mph) than the Tiger Moths we'd flown at Grading School. He also wished us the best of luck and the usual service reminder to behave ourselves. I believe his actual admonition, delivered with typical Canadian candour was, 'You play ball with us, or I'll stick the bat and ball where it hurts most!'

We were naturally keen to get cracking and our training got under way. It followed the tried and tested pattern of dividing the course into two sections, one flying during the morning session, while the other attended lectures on the associated flying subjects. In the afternoon the roles were reversed. Each flying instructor was responsible for training two students in each section. My instructor was a Canadian, F/O Bill Robinson, not much older than myself and we soon established a rapport. The weather was excellent and afforded uninterrupted flying instruction and I had no problems getting the hang of the Cornell, so it wasn't long before I soloed. When I did, the euphoria hit me once again and confirmed the belief that from now on I was on my own and it was up to me to make the most of it – I was 'captain of my fate'!

One amusing aspect of the flying was that when we took off and landed we had an audience of gophers (North American ground squirrels) which inhabited warrens near the landing strip. They would sit by the strip on their haunches watching the proceedings, their heads moving to and fro just like a Wimbledon crowd watching the tennis.

The Cornell was a good training aircraft but it had its idiosyncrasies, one of which occurred sometimes during spinning, when the spin flattened and stabilised, thus presenting difficulties for recovery. We were briefed if this occurred and normal recovery hadn't been achieved after four turns, that we were to bale out!

Consequently I recall that on my first solo spinning detail I climbed the Cornell up to 5,000 feet then having second thoughts I took it up another 1,000 – just in case. After levelling off, I carried out my pre-spin checks meticulously, then throttled back, eased back on the stick and the juddering commenced as the stall approached. I pulled the stick fully back and applied full left rudder. Over she went and the spin commenced. After three turns I applied full opposite (right) rudder easing the stick forward at the same time. To my relief after another two turns the spin stopped. I centralised the controls and applied power to regain the height I'd lost. As this was my first solo spin, I can say that a certain amount of adrenalin was on the move! However, after a short while flying straight and level and with my confidence established, I carried on spinning and recovering. On completion of the sortie when I landed back at base, to say I was feeling pretty chuffed would be an under-statement.

My training progressed favourably both in the air and on the ground. I passed all my progress checks during the various stages of the course, general handling, pilot navigation and flying on instruments. I found that pilot navigation in the west of Canada wasn't too difficult as the fences dividing the farmland sections, run north/south and east/west, so with a map and a serviceable compass, it was easy to orient oneself. Also at every town rail-head, the storage grain elevator had the name of the town emblazoned on its roof.

The introduction to basic aerobatics was interesting and exhilarating. As my previous flying as aircrew had been in heavy multi-engined aircraft, the nearest I'd come to aerobatics was on operations doing violent manoeuvres such as steep turns, spiral dives and some inadvertent stalls! However after being upside down a few times I was able to cope, even if I did stall on the top of the odd loop.

Our low-flying area was to the south of Assiniboia near the United States border which we sometimes 'accidentally' infringed. I had always enjoyed low-flying, even in the heavies, but in a small aircraft such as the Cornell it was even better. My instructor also introduced me to spotting and 'buzzing' coyotes which inhabited the area – I can imagine the present-day animal rights enthusiasts throwing up their arms in horror, but it was only an expression of our youthful high spirits and I'm sure the extra running we inflicted on the coyotes did them no real harm.

The course wasn't all work and no play. During our off-duty weekends we had the opportunity to explore the local countryside and the local town of Assininboia in particular. It was a real western Canadian one-horse town. It had dirt streets with wooden side-walks and one hotel, the El Prada, which the Assiniboia flyers had re-named the El Prango! At weekends dances were held there during which some of the 'fly boys' attempted to impress the local talent with their *Palais de Danse* ability. Suffice to say that the joint was far from static by the end of the evening!

The good weather continued through the summer of 1944 allowing unrestricted flying instruction and before we knew it, final ground and flying checks were upon us. During the lead-up, progress checks had resulted in a certain amount of wastage and some of our unfortunate fellow students who had failed the checks had left us to be re-graded. Those of us who were left and who had successfully completed the final tests now awaited our postings. Throughout our training our flying potential had been assessed and a decision made as to whether the 'Advanced' phase of our training would be on twin or single-engine aircraft. Most of us saw ourselves as future Spitfire aces of course, but the powers that be had the last word. It did my ego no harm whatsoever when I learned that I was to continue my training on singles.

Those selected for training on twins were posted after a short leave to their respective

Advanced Flying Training Schools, without delay, but our posting to the Harvard (single-engine) AFTSs was delayed. This turned out to be a blessing in disguise, as it allowed a sergeant cadet friend, Paddy McKay and myself to accept an invitation from one of our flying instructors, Pete Canavan (an American in the RCAF) to spend our leave with him and his family in St Louis.

It was a never to be forgotten holiday during which we sampled American hospitality and friendship. It gave us the opportunity of mixing and talking with Americans in their own backyard. A highlight of our stay was a trip down the great River Mississippi in a vintage paddle-steamer.

Throughout our stay we were given VIP treatment – 'Say; you're English, speak some English!' We were very sorry when our leave ended and we had to return to Assiniboia. When we got back we were informed that there was still a hold-up in our posting to AFTS, but to keep us out of mischief, the SNCO ex-aircrew cadets were to go to a Bombing and Gunnery School at Picton, Ontario. There they made use of our previous operational experience by employing us to instruct in Bombing and Gunnery both in the classroom and in the air.

Picton wasn't far from the city of Toronto which we were able to visit and sample its sights and 'diversions'.

Eventually our enforced instructional detachment ended and we were posted to a single-engine AFTS. I was most pleased to discover that I was to go RCAF Uplands, not far from the capital city of Ottawa.

When we arrived at RCAF Uplands, after being allocated our accommodation and settling in we were welcomed by the CO and his training staff, who explained the training procedure particular to Uplands and the usual do's and don'ts with regard to behaviour on and off duty.

Our training was to follow the usual pattern of flying instruction supplemented with classroom lectures on all the associated aviation subjects.

Ever since being informed that I would be continuing my training on singles, I'd looked forward to flying the famous North American Harvard single-engined trainer, noted for the noisy rasping sound of its engine caused by its propeller tips exceeding the speed of sound. It nevertheless had the reputation of being an excellent advanced trainer. Powered by a 550hp Pratt and Whitney Wasp engine, which gave it a top speed of 205mph at 5,000 feet and a cruising speed of 170mph, it met all the requirements for advance single-engine training.

After a flight to familiarise us with the surrounding area, especially the prohibited areas such as the city of nearby Ottawa, training started in earnest. My instructor, another Canadian Flying Officer, by the name of McLean, was very proud of his Scottish ancestry. He was a few years older than myself and because of his premature baldness he was lumbered with the inevitable nom de plume, not by me of course – I wanted to keep in his good books, so the nearest I got to familiarity was to address him as 'Mac'.

Flying the Harvard met all the expectations I'd dreamed of over the years when I was aspiring to get to the sharp end. It had, like every other aircraft, distinct characteristics, for instance I soon learned of its tendency to 'ground loop' if three-point landings were attempted in cross-wind conditions and to 'flick' into spins if roughly handled at low speeds.

Depending on ability, solo standard was achieved after about six to eight hours dual flying. However there were some students who didn't make it despite extra tuition and were posted for reselection. I'm glad to say that, with the help of Mac, I coped and progressed through the various stages – 'circuits and bumps' including power-on and power-off (glide) approaches, normal, flapless, precautionary (short) take-offs and landings and simulated engine failure after take-off (forced landings). I enjoyed every minute of it, especially when we left the circuit for the advanced stages which included stalling, spinning and eventually aerobatics, formation flying, pilot navigation and instrument flying. We were subjected to progress flying checks at every stage and periodic ground school examinations with the possibility (perish the thought) of being scrubbed if we failed to make the grade.

After successfully achieving the required standard of day flying we were then introduced to night flying. My previous night flying experience in the black-out conditions in the UK and other parts of Europe stood me in good stead and also the unrestricted lighting in Canada made night flying a much easier proposition.

One of our solo night navigation exercises was a triangular cross-country and mine took place on a beautiful, cold, starlit night with excellent visibility. I took off from Uplands and climbed on course for my first turning point which was the large crucifix monument at the top of a hill near the city of Montreal. The monument was brilliantly lit and the visibility was so good I could see it when I was miles away. It was a magnificent sight which I'll always remember. On reaching it I turned onto my next leg which led me down the St Lawrence river towards Kingston. Again I had no trouble seeing the next turning point or finding my way from there back to base, all in all a really enjoyable experience.

Our Harvard training took place during the winter of 1944. Canadian winters follow a predictable timetable and we awoke one morning to discover everything covered in a blanket of blinding white snow. Soon snow-blowers were in operation clearing the runways, throwing the snow to build up banks at each side. Subsequent falls were rolled and packed down on the runway to give a level surface. The result was a long narrow skating-rink which required special handling techniques during taxiing, take-offs and landings, to avoid skating into the snow banks and parked aircraft. Most of us coped, however one unfortunate solo student – who forgot about the ineffectiveness of his brakes – taxied back to the parking apron and inadvertently chewed up the tail of the aircraft parked in front of him!

I found that flying in the winter conditions was a delight. On most days there were cloudless skies and the unlimited visibility presented me with the opportunity during solo sorties to attempt to emulate my instructor's proficiency at aerobatics. His forte was eight point 'hesitation' rolls and rolls off the top of loops. I didn't manage to reach his standard but had a great time trying, despite some inadvertent stalling and spinning!

The course progressed to its ultimate goal, the final qualifying Wings Check. I'll never forget the feeling of pleasure I experienced when the Chief Instructor said to me when we landed after he had put me through the hoop, 'Yes, I guess you'll do.' I contained my exuberance until I got back to the crew-room, then it hit me, I'd made it and achieved what I'd promised myself as a boy. Later I joined my other successful Wings Check colleagues in a small celebration.

After all the students had their Wings Check, those who had been successful were sent from Uplands to Carp, an airfield some twenty-five miles away to carry out armament training, which comprised dive and low-level bombing using $4\frac{1}{2}$lb practice bombs, air to ground live firing using the single fixed .303 Browning machine-gun fitted to the Harvard, and air to air camera gun exercises.

We received dual instruction before being sent on solo sorties and bombing exercises were carried out using as a target a ring of small fir trees embedded in the ice on a nearby frozen lake. Low level attacks were supposed to be carried out from nought feet indicated on the altimeter with a standard setting (actual height 200 feet) but on our solo exercises I think most of us bent the rules and attacked from lower altitudes, despite risking the censure of the Officer I/C bomb plotting. Low flying had always given me a buzz and I made the most of the opportunity to do it officially.

Dive-bombing was carried out commencing the dive from 2,500 feet and releasing the bomb at 800 feet, following the approved procedure, i.e. approach the range straight and level at 2,500 feet and after obtaining permission to commence the exercise, identify the target and assess the wind direction from a smoke-flare on the range. Fly parallel to the target at 2,500 feet, then do a wing-over into the dive, positioning the target on the relevant part of the upper engine cowling, depending on the wind direction, e.g. left, centre or right (very primitive!) then release the bomb at the required altitude. This could be a bit tricky as the bomb-release button in the Harvard was tucked away in the top left corner of the instrument panel. After release the procedure was to pull out of the dive into a climbing turn to observe the bomb burst.

One of my solo dive-bombing sorties unfortunately did not go as planned. The visibility on this occasion was affected by the odd snow flurry, but I carried out the recognised procedure, identifying what I assumed was the target and assessing the wind etc., then commenced my wing-over and endeavoured to position the target on the relevant part of the engine-cowling. However, to my surprise the target moved away. What I had assumed was the target turned out to be a group of men who had trespassed onto the range and were busily engaged in illegally cutting ice from the frozen lake. I hastily pulled out of my dive – the ice thieves would have been more than surprised if I'd lobbed a smoke bomb among them. I then informed the Range Officer who cancelled my detail until he sorted out the miscreants!

Air-to-air camera-gun exercises comprised simulated fighter attacks from various sectors, e.g. bow, beam and quarter on a target aircraft flying in a prescribed area on a steady course (tow-line), the camera recording the results. After landing the film was processed, the results assessed and shown to the pilot at de-briefing.

The air-to-ground live firing was a dual-only exercise. I suppose the powers that be were carefully avoiding the possibility of our erratic marksmanship, or trigger-happy exuberance. They were well aware of the ambition of all to become Spitfire aces!

Our course flying instruction had, up to now, been free from serious accidents, but unfortunately during our Armament School sojourn we suffered our first and only fatality. I witnessed it at first hand. I was waiting behind another aircraft to take-off on an air-to-air camera-gun sortie when an aircraft on a long final approach to land was intercepted by another doing a very tight circuit. The student pilot of this aircraft was obviously under the impression he could turn onto finals and land in front of the other aircraft. As he came cross-wind and commenced a steep turn onto finals the two aircraft were on a collision course. The pilots must have seen each other simultaneously. The one on long finals poured on full power and climbed away to the right. The other attempted to climb away steeply to the left, but stalled, flicked into a spin and crashed short of the runway.

All aircraft waiting to take-off were instructed to hold their position as the ambulance and crash-tender sped to the scene. After a short time they left the area and we were informed that flying was to recommence. We were given permission to take-off in turn and I should imagine that the accident we had witnessed certainly concentrated our minds. I know it did mine and I recall that during my camera-gun exercise I did everything as per the book. When I landed back at base I was informed that our student colleague had been killed in the crash. Needless to say it had a very sobering effect on us and I think we were all ultra-careful during the remainder of our course. Thankfully there were no more such incidents and when our armament training was successfully completed we returned to Uplands for the Wings Parade ceremony. Some of us were informed that we would also receive our commissions. Being a peacetime regular airman I had, like most regulars, looked upon the wartime practice of awarding commissions to aircrew on completion of their flying training with a certain amount of derisory reserve, being of the jaundiced opinion that some of them had neither service experience nor the maturity to merit the responsibility. However, being in the frame now myself I could no longer comment, but I smugly convinced myself that I could not be described as 'jumped up' by the old sweats!

By this time, March 1945, Allied air superiority in Europe had been established and, as sufficient fully trained aircrew replacements were now available, it was decided that the Commonwealth Air Training Scheme should be run down. An official closing ceremony was organised to take place at RCAF Uplands during which a selected member of each aircrew category and nationality graduating from training schools in Canada, would be presented with their brevets. So instead of taking part in my course presentation of wings, I was held back and selected to be the RAF pilot representative at the official closing down ceremony.

After numerous rehearsals, the 'Big Day' arrived, but unfortunately adverse weather made it impossible for the ceremony to be held outdoors, so it was held in an aircraft hangar. High-ranking representatives of all the Allied Governments and Air Forces who had been involved with the Air Training Scheme assembled in the hangar to witness the proceedings. Somebody commented that there was so much top brass attending, they were employing Group Captains as car-park attendants!

When the proceedings got under way all the fortunate graduates were marched into the hangar and formed up in front of the seated celebrities. Then as our names, nationality and aircrew category was called out, we marched smartly to the presentation dais, where we were given our brevets and congratulations by the presenting officer, His Excellency, the Governor General of Canada, the Earl of Athlone. One of my proudest possessions is a photograph of His Excellency pinning on my pilot's wings.

I was now a fully-fledged member of the 'Driver-airframe' fraternity. As well as

Governor General of Canada presents pilots' wings to Larry Donnelly, March 1945.

receiving my wings, I also received my commission. I recall that during the reception held after the ceremony, the Station Commander (a RAF Group Captain) pulled my leg, pointing out that I was no longer a 'king-pin' (Warrant Officer) in the Sergeants' Mess, but now the lowest form of life (Pilot Officer) in the Officers' Mess. I assured him that having eventually achieved my boyhood ambition to become a pilot in the Royal Air Force was sufficient compensation for losing my so-called king-pin status.

And so, my training successfully completed, I entered the repatriation 'sausage machine' to return to the UK. I bade farewell to RCAF Uplands and the beautiful city of Ottawa and proceeded by train to the port of Halifax, Nova Scotia, where I boarded the SS *Aquitania*, another of the pre-war ocean greyhounds that had been pressed into service as a troopship.

It was packed to the gunwales with servicemen, the Air Force personnel being out-numbered by the reinforcements for the Canadian Army invasion forces. There were so many on board that we had sleep and eat in shifts! Again like our outbound voyage to New York, we were unescorted, relying on speed to foil any marauding U-boats, although that menace had been considerably reduced by this stage of the war.

The voyage, uncomfortable, but thankfully uneventful, was accepted by the RAF personnel without many complaints, despite the fact that we were going back to rationing and black-out. The big bonus was that we were returning to our loved ones who we hadn't seen for some time.

We eventually arrived safely at Greenock, where we disembarked. After clearing customs, the RAF contingent boarded trains to take them to Reception Centres. The depot for commissioned RAF aircrew was at Harrogate where we were billeted in commandeered hotels. After going through the booking in procedure we were given fourteen days leave, during which I was able to distribute the goodies I'd brought from Canada. It was amazing in those days what nylon stockings could do for your popularity!

My leave passed far too quickly and I returned to Harrogate where I found it was Heaton-Park all over again – organised chaos! To keep us occupied we were sent on various courses ranging from Junior Officers' Administration to Ship Recognition. However some of us were fortunate to get a short detachment to an EFTS where we flew Tiger Moths.

By this time the conflict in Europe was drawing to its close, so the training to provide replacements and reinforcements slowed and consequently my chances of continuing operational training were also affected. After achieving my ambition to get my wings, it now looked as if my flying career as pilot might be moribund – but not if I had anything to do with it!

A Fairchild Cornell.

Larry Donnelly flies a Harvard in formation.

Twelve
In Limbo

After VE and VJ days, training virtually ceased and the Demob machinery got under way. It was a case of 'first in first out', and as I was a pre-war regular airman I could have been among the first to be demobbed had I desired, however having eventually achieved my ambition to be a pilot as well as being commissioned I wanted to stay in the RAF and fly. I also surmised that out in civvy street there would be flocks of experienced wartime pilots endeavouring to get into civil flying, so I didn't fancy my chances. When I was interviewed I made my wishes known to the Demob Panel, but I was told that I'd have to wait and see how things panned out.

The only cheerful event that occurred at the time was that my old oppo Chas Armstrong reappeared on the scene. After we had parted company in 1942, he'd gone to RAF Bowmore to a newly formed Sunderland Squadron, but unfortunately before they could get operational all their boats had been swamped in a terrific storm, so he had ended up in West Africa on another Sunderland squadron with whom he'd flown another tour. By now he, like myself, had been commissioned. He was now back at No. 1 Electrical and Wireless School, RAF Cranwell, on a technical signals officers' course. We naturally had a great reunion. Our wives met for the first time and subsequently they too became firm friends.

In August 1945, I was posted to the Aircrew Holding Unit at RAF Pembrey in South Wales where I was given the job of Adjutant to the CO W/Cdr Carron. There were literally hundreds of aircrew awaiting their turn to go to the Demob Centres. Because of the limited accommodation we had a hot bed situation which was only relieved by sending them on 'accommodation leave' in rotation. In between times we had to keep them occupied/entertained and out of mischief. It was an uphill task, which taxed the ingenuity of Wing Commander Carron and myself to the limit. We organised visits to places which we thought might arouse their interest. One, to the Carmarthen Assizes was particularly popular, especially if there were any juicy cases being heard. I also managed to get in touch via Air Ministry, with a film distributor in Wardour Street, London who loaned us a variety of films, mostly foreign made. An explosives factory at nearby 'Slash' (Llanelly) was also on the visiting list, as well as the Army Experimental Firing Range at Pendine, where they used captured German armour as targets.

By the beginning of 1946 I thought it was time to move on and began making enquiries about my chances of getting back into the air again, flying as pilot, but without any success. During one of my 'moans' to the Wing Commander I mentioned that to get back into the air I was even prepared to fly in my previous capacity as Wireless Operator.

I was working on the premise I might be able to influence a speedy return to the sharp end. Let's face it, I had no ambition to continue as a mahogany bomber (desk) pilot. The CO was most sympathetic and promised to see what he could do. The result was that out of the blue I was granted an interview at Transport Command Headquarters, Bushey Park, where I did my utmost to impress the Command Signals Officer that I was still capable of key bashing. To my delight and astonishment he believed me!

The outcome was a posting on a quick refresher course after which I was posted to No. 51 Squadron an ex-4 Group Halifax Squadron, now with Transport Command, to fly as wireless operator. This was a far cry from my ambition to become a Spitfire pilot but beggars can't be choosers. My arrival caused quite a stir especially among the Wireless Operating fraternity when it was realised a pilot was joining them. However they welcomed me into the fold and later on I think they were suitably impressed when I managed a Wireless Operator 'B' category from the 'Trappers' (the Transport Command Examining Board).

The squadron aircrew were practically all ex-bomber boys. The CO was W/Cdr 'Hank' Iveson DSO DFC, with whom I'd served on 76 Squadron in 1941. Another ex-Bomber character was Flt Lt Stu' Sloan CGM, who was awarded his gong as a navigator/bomb-aimer when he flew his damaged Wellington back from Germany after his pilot had baled out! He had subsequently remustered as pilot and was now flying in that capacity. His career as pilot prospered and he eventually went as pilot/captain in the Royal Flight.

51 Squadron, based at RAF Stradishall was in the process of converting onto Avro Yorks and I joined a crew captained by Flt Lt Nash. We carried out our conversion at the satellite RAF Wratting Common. To begin with my operating technique was a bit rusty, but I managed to cope and passed my categorisation check. Soon after our successful conversion we commenced flying the long-range Transport Command routes.

Our first flight was to Palam (Delhi) staging through Castel-Benito (Tripoli) – El Adem – Almaza (Cairo) – Shaibah (Iraq) – Mauripur (Karachi) – Palam. This was my first flight to the Middle East and India and it was a fascinating experience, being able to fly over and to land at places which up to then, for me, had been place-names on a map, or the subject of line-shoots by old sweats who had served in the Middle or Far East. Unfortunately the schedule didn't allow much time for sight seeing but I appreciated having the sun on my back for a change. The 1946/47 winter was the worst for years. Some villages in the UK were snowed in, so in between route flying the squadron was employed in dropping much needed supplies to them.

Not only did route flying give us the chance to get some short relief from the arctic weather conditions in the UK it also gave us the opportunity to obtain, from the various stops en route, items unavailable or on ration in the UK. After nearly six years of war, rationing and austerity, it was, to use an old barrack-room expression, a chance to fill our boots. We were able to get commodities which for us at that time were luxuries, such as tinned food which was unobtainable and items of clothing that were coupon rationed.

All our purchases overseas had to be declared on return to the customs in the UK and dutiable goods were charged. This was accepted by most of the law-abiding crews, but human nature being what it is there were few of us who could not resist the temptation to do a bit of surreptitious smuggling. I suppose the risk of being caught by the customs also provided a bit of excitement to keep the adrenalin going. There were however some who tended to over do it, endeavouring to make a fast buck by exploiting the various shortages – smuggling in large amounts to flog on the black market at home.

Our main task during this period was to bring servicemen from overseas to the UK for demobilisation and to fly out the replacements considered necessary. Flying over vast expanses of land and sea in tropical meteorological conditions was a completely new and fascinating experience for me, especially during the monsoon seasons, when we were at the mercy of the elements, which could make things a bit dicey at times. One occasion when we were flying the Habbaniya to Karachi leg, in the vicinity of the Persian Gulf at 7,000 feet, we were sucked into a towering cumulo-nimbus cloud and spewed out of it, at 17,000 feet, seconds later. After we had simmered down we checked for damage and were concerned to discover that the centre stabiliser between the two tail-fins was missing. It says a lot for the design of the Avro York (which was developed from the Avro Lancaster) that the flying characteristics weren't seriously affected, mind you we were ultra careful for the rest of the flight and landing at Karachi. Apparently our arrival in the circuit caused some confusion with regard to aircraft recognition by the onlookers – 'It's a Lanc, no it's a York.' We were AOG (aircraft on ground) until repairs were carried out. A consolation was that we had some extra shopping time!

On another trip when we stopped at Dum Dum (Calcutta) on our way to Singapore, I met a previous acquaintance. When we landed we were met by the Station Commander, who turned out to be Gp Capt L.S. Snaith with whom I had served during 1940/41 when he was Wing Commander, CO of 19 OTU. During a conversation in the mess later, I recalled the last time I'd seen him was when he carpeted Chas Armstrong and myself for fiddling our posting on a second bomber tour, ignoring his official channels. I don't know if he remembered the incident but he commented he was pleased that our luck had held out and we'd survived. He was also interested to see that my attempts to remuster as pilot had been successful, but sorry to see that I'd had to revert to wireless operating again to remain flying. On that occasion our departure from Dum Dum was delayed when we were informed our aircraft was unserviceable. The Group Captain commiserated and suggested that while we waited for our aircraft to become serviceable, we could go down the River Hooghli in the Station's boat and visit the famous Calcutta botanical gardens, where a banyan tree, reputed to be the largest tree in the world, existed. It was an offer we thought we couldn't refuse!

So the next day after a leisurely breakfast we set off in the boat and disembarked at the gardens where we commenced our tour. Unfortunately when we were halfway through our sightseeing, the heavens opened and the rain came down in torrents. Bearers carried us back to the boat on their backs – the paths having become rivers. When we got back to Dum Dum we found that our rooms were flooded. Luckily we had been advised to put our suitcases on the top of the wardrobes so our kit was dry, but our beds were floating! In the Officers' Mess the bearers were using mosquito nets to trawl the marine and animal life – fish, reptiles etc. It was subsequently calculated that eleven and a half inches of rain had fallen during the space of a few hours.

During another UK to Singapore flight (using the southern route, via Karachi and

Negombo (Ceylon – now Sri Lanka) we again suffered damage from the effects of cu nims. This time hailstones as big as ping-pong balls cracked the windscreen and dented the mainplane and tailplane leading edges. We were AOG at Negombo for three weeks because spares had to be obtained from the makers in the UK. It was no hardship for us – we were able to bask in the sun, swim in the Indian Ocean and explore the city of Colombo. Monsoon flying did have its compensations!

By this time the squadron had moved from Stradishall to Waterbeach near Cambridge. I managed to obtain living-out accommodation in the nearby village of Trumpington from where I commuted to and from Waterbeach on my bike. The living-in boys used the same form of transport when they missed the last bus from Cambridge after carousing at their favourite watering hole, the Baron of Beef, but unfortunately the bikes they used tended to be commandeered from students without their knowledge! One night one of these bike thieves was weaving his way back to camp on a commandeered bike when he was stopped by the local policeman near Waterbeach who had the task of curbing these thefts. The policeman asked him to confirm that the bike belonged to him. He said it did, so the policeman then asked him what make it was. Having taken it in the dark he hadn't a clue what it was, but he crossed his fingers and said it was a Raleigh – the policeman shone his torch on it and to the surprise of both of them it really was a Raleigh! He thought he'd got away with it but realised the game was up when the policeman asked him why he had bought a ladies' model! To combat these activities the police carried out surprise searches at Waterbeach with the Station Commander's permission and transported recovered bikes back to their rightful owners.

I continued flying with the squadron as wireless operator until the end of April 1947,

Avro York.

when I was given the welcome news that I was to resume my post-graduate pilot training. I had enjoyed route flying and I will always remember the awe-inspiring sight of cu nims towering up to 40 and 50,000 feet, over Malaya and Sumatra, as we flew down the Malacca straits to Singapore and also the dicey crossings of the Bay of Bengal at night as we flew through the monsoon storms, but I couldn't wait to get my sticky fingers on the pole again.

Before I left Waterbeach, I was given further good news – I had been granted an Extended Service Commission 'B' which meant I could serve for a further twelve years, with a pension at the end of it. The Station Commander advised me to accept it, as it was a step towards a permanent commission. I acted on his advice – I couldn't pass up the opportunity of another twelve years flying now could I?

Thirteen
Refreshed – Back To The Sharp End

I got one or two surprises when I reported to Moreton (Much Binding) in-Marsh to commence the pilot refresher course. The first was that I would be flying Air-speed Oxford (twin-engine) training aircraft. Having been trained on Harvard (single-engine) trainers I had hoped that I would continue on singles, but having eventually got back to the sharp end I wasn't going to rock the boat.

The second, more pleasant surprise was that among the twenty pilots on the course were two officers with whom I'd served previously on operational squadrons when I was a WOp/AG. The first was Max Nixon, a New Zealander who had flown with No. 10 (Whitley) Squadron at the same time as myself (1939/40). He had been the captain of an aircraft which had failed to return from a raid on the Zeiss works at Jena on the 16/17 August 1940. His aircraft had crashed at Zeugenbergen in Holland. He and his crew escaped serious injury, but they were captured while attempting to escape. While they were on the run, the BBC announced that the Germans were offering a reward for their capture. They were 'banged up' for the duration and repatriated when hostilities ended. F/O Nixon had been progressively promoted during his incarceration and was now a Squadron Leader.

The other officer, S/Ldr W.R. Williams was on No. 76 (Halifax) Squadron when I was on my second bomber tour. He had been shot down (damaged by flak and attacks by Me109s) and ditched off La Rochelle on the squadron's ill-fated raid on the German battleship *Scharnhorst* berthed at La Pallice in July 1941. He and his crew were captured and incarcerated until the end of the war.

Most of the officers on the course were ex-'Kreigies'. Another, S/Ldr P.G. (Butch) Brodie, had been captain of a 51 Squadron Whitley, which had crash-landed in Holland after being badly damaged by flak while attacking a power station at Schornewitz on 19/20 August 1940. He and his crew had escaped unhurt but were captured.

Another was S/Ldr 'Skid' Morley, an ex-Hampden skipper who was lucky to be alive. During a raid in 1940, his aircraft had received a direct hit from flak and exploded. He was the only survivor of his crew. After having been blown out of the Hampden, he recovered consciousness to find himself dangling on the end of his pilot type parachute which had opened on its own when he was blown out of the aircraft. While in the 'bag' he had attempted another escape when doing some tunnelling. He and his fellow would-be

Airspeed 'Oxfords' Refresher Course.

escapees inadvertently broke through into a disused latrine – the cry went up, 'Back boys, were in the s★★t!'

S/Ldr 'Fairey' Fairbanks was a pilot who had been shot down during the Battle of France in 1940. When he was repatriated at the end of the war, he, like the others, had received a wad of back pay. He apparently took off on a spending spree, only returning to his unit when his finances were running very low. When asked what he had done with all of his back pay, his reply was, 'Well, you know how it goes; wine, fast women, slow horses and I guess I must have squandered the rest!'

So you can imagine that life in the Officers' Mess at Much Binding was quite hectic. Every other night was party night, with the 'Wild Bunch' being led by W/Cdr Lynch Blosse, the OC Flying Wing who was also an ex-PoW. I was fortunate to escape when I managed to get some accommodation and commenced living out at a nearby town, managing to avoid most of the festivities. However, when the 'Wild Bunch' came to town I was sometimes conscripted and lumbered with providing midnight snacks!

Flying the Oxford was interesting and initially posed some problems for me, but I coped and enjoyed both the day and night flying. After night flying, cycling back home in the early dawn could also cause problems. The area was subject to early marsh mists and I recall it was quite weird having to pedal along the country lanes with only my head and shoulders out of the mist, endeavouring to keep on the road by keeping equi-distant between the hedgerows. I suppose I was fortunate, because at that time of the morning the roads were generally deserted.

Having now become proficient on 'twins' I presumed I'd be posted to a multi-engined squadron in Bomber, Coastal or Transport command, but instead at the end of the course I was posted to 695 Army/Navy co-operation Squadron in Fighter command, at Horsham-St-Faiths, near Norwich. I was a bit confused – having been initially trained on

Miles Martinet.

singles, I was then given a refresher on twins to find I'd been posted to a predominantly singles squadron!

The squadron was equipped with Spitfire Mk XVIs (modified Mk IXs with clipped wings and powered by Packard Merlins), Miles Martinets and Airspeed Oxfords. A detachment of three Spitfires, two Martinets and two Oxfords was based at Wattisham and I was sent there initially to fly the Oxfords.

On joining the detachment I found that the Spitfires were used in the Naval co-operation role, carrying out low-level simulated torpedo attacks on RN destroyers operating out of Sheerness. The Martinet was used to tow targets for the Army ack ack units on the east coast and the Oxfords were used for Naval radar development.

I found that flying on the radar development task could be quite enjoyable. As we carried no navigators we had to do our own pilot navigation and to rely on the Naval radar for precise course and altitude control. On getting airborne on a detail R/T contact would be established with the Navy Controller and as soon as he had confirmed positive radar contact, he would pass courses and altitudes to fly, the object being to calibrate the exact range and altitude at which they lost radar contact. This sometimes involved flying at low-level over designated prohibited areas, e.g. the city of London, and, for range calibration flying, towards France and Belgium and descending to establish the exact range and altitude the aircraft blip disappeared from the radar screen. This added a bit of a fillip as it provided the opportunity to officially fly at very low level along the French and Belgian beaches and eyeball the local female sunbathers!

The Martinet task was much more mundane, flying up and down a designated tow-line towing a drogue while the Army ack ack gunners attempted to improve their marksmanship. On one such detail, the Martinet with drogue streamed was stooging up the tow-line when a burst of ack ack appeared not too far in front of the aircraft. The pilot's immediate reaction was to release the drogue, take evasive action and to inform the ack ack controller on the R/T that he had been pulling the bloody drogue, not pushing it!

The Spitfire details were the most exciting, involving very low flying simulating torpedo attacks against the naval destroyers off Sheerness, however on occasion the unexpected hiccup could occur, as happened during one sortie which was being witnessed by some visiting top naval brass assembled at the end of a jetty at Sheerness.

The Spitfire pilot in the process of carrying out his simulated attack, descended to sea level hopping over the destroyer after his simulated drop. He continued flying at sea level before pulling up into a steep climb over the assembled spectators on the jetty. Apparently the party was standing too close to the edge and as the Spitfire zoomed over, one heavily be-decked Admiral swivelled round, over-balanced and plunged into the oggin!

By the time the aircraft landed back at Wattisham the telephone lines were buzzing. The irate, wringing wet Admiral was demanding the pilot's head on a plate. However, our tactful flight commander was able mollify his indignation and no further action was taken. During a subsequent telephone conversation the captain of the destroyer commented that it couldn't have happened to a nicer bloke!

After I'd settled in and been with the detachment for a while I was checked out first on the Martinet and then on the Spitfire – I'd made it at last. My first flight in the Spitfire was unforgettable and to say I reached cloud nine would be an under-statement. Mind you my first take-off viewed from the ground apparently followed a beginner's usual pattern. There was a distinct 'jink' when I changed hands from the throttle to the stick to raise the undercarriage, and my first landing could have been smoother; however as far as I was concerned, the euphoria I felt compensated for any criticism.

Our detachment at Wattisham had no facilities for major servicing, so whenever an

Spitfire Mark XVI.

aircraft became due for a major inspection, it was ferried back to our home base of Horsham-St-Faiths. It was a deliver and collect system, to fit in with the servicing schedule. The ferrying was on a rota, which allowed the pilots on detachment to meet up with our fellow pilots at Horsham, and get the latest gen and have a night out in Norwich at the Samson and Hercules Club (nicknamed The Muscle Club by the Horsham fly boys).

I recall on one of my ferry trips I was with oppos waiting in the mess lounge for lunch, when one of our pilots came in with our squadron mascot, a large Irish Wolfhound called Bruce. He told me he had been lumbered with the task of mascot minder. This had come about because of Bruce's favourite pastime of chasing the aircraft as they taxied out to fly. The Station Commander saw him and 'lowered the boom'. He got in touch with our CO and told him to 'get that so-and-so on a lead and kept under control.'

The next time he visited our squadron, he was looking out of the window when our mascot minder passed. He smiled at the CO and held up the piece of rope he was holding. Puzzled the Station Commander watched as twenty yards of rope passed by with a very dejected Irish Wolfhound on the end of it.

The boss appreciated the humour commenting, 'It wasn't what I had in mind, but at least it might stop him from being chopped up, or sucked in and incinerated!'

I continued flying with the detachment until February 1948 when I was sent to an operational conversion unit (OCU) to convert onto Hornets (the single-seat fighter version of the Mosquito). The Hornet at that time had the reputation of being able to leave most of the current piston-engine fighters standing, so I looked forward to my conversion. Sadly, things didn't turn out as planned. When I arrived at the OCU, I was informed that the one and only aircraft had been written-off and I was to return to my unit. This I did, fed up and frustrated. My CO was sympathetic, but there was nothing he could do about it, so I went back to continue flying with the squadron detachment and await further developments.

It wasn't all gloom – in June 1948 our daughter was born, so that brought me pleasantly down to earth and I was checked out as a PPP (Proud Pram Pusher).

However, back into the air and after a few months I came to the conclusion my flying career was in the doldrums, so when the Russians lowered the boom and the Berlin Air Lift commenced, I volunteered to return to Transport Command. To my surprise I was granted an interview at Transport Command HQ where I was offered and accepted the opportunity to train in the Medium Range role as an aircraft captain. However, I was informed that as the Air Lift was in progress I would have to wait for my conversion course. In the meantime I was posted to RAF Lyneham Air Movements and detached to RAF Buckeburg in Germany.

So off I went to the Berlin Air Lift and it proved to be a very interesting experience. Our aircraft operated out of ex-Luftwaffe bases, Yorks out of Wunsdorf and Dakotas out of Buckeburg and I managed to scrounge the odd trip to Gatow (Berlin) with the Dakota squadron.

The weather conditions were atrocious at times and the aircraft on arrival at Gatow were stacked at separation levels to take their turn to be fed into the Ground Control Approach (GCA) pattern for landing. On one occasion a York crew was at the top of the

Pilot's Refresher Course.

stack and had to hold for some considerable time. After a while, the captain, obviously fed-up with orbiting, is reputed to have called Gatow Tower on the R/T: 'Hello Gatow, this is Mike Oboe Yoke Able Victor, orbiting at 15,000 feet. I hope you realise down there I'm only on a short service commission!'

After a few months I was recalled to the UK and posted to North Luffenham on a Medium Range (Dakota) Captains' Course, followed by a Transport Support Course at Netheravon where I was introduced to the technique of carrying and dropping paratroops, airborne supplies and towing gliders. This latter (towing gliders) could, at Netheravon, be a bit of a tricky business especially at night. Even at this late stage (1949) Netheravon was still a grass airfield with a prominent hump running across it. Consequently on take-off you could only see the first half of the goose-neck flare-path until you got over the hump. It could be quite fraught, if when you got to the hump, the glider got airborne in a 'high tow' attitude, which resulted in raising the Dakota's tail preventing it from getting airborne before the end of the flare-path. The glider pilots were warned of this and informed that if such a situation came about the glider would be cast off – released prematurely; not a very safe proposition at night!

Fortunately no such incidents occurred during the course which I completed successfully in July 1949. I was then sent on embarkation leave prior to being posted to join 114 Squadron, a Dakota squadron at RAF Kabrit in the Suez Canal zone.

Fourteen
Getting My Knees Brown

My embarkation leave was cut short by a terse signal from Air Ministry instructing me to report to the PDC (Personnel Dispatch Centre) in London, with kit, but to wear civilian clothes. During my journey to London I racked my brains attempting to solve the reason for the unusual directive concerning my having to wear my civvies, instead of uniform.

All was revealed when I reported to the PDC, where the Movements Officer informed me that three other officers (one other pilot and two navigators), who had already reported, and myself were to fly to Cairo the following day by the Dutch Airline KLM, then travel by train to the Canal Zone. When I pointed out that I didn't have a passport, he told that me arrangements had been made so that we could use our F's1250 (RAF Identification cards) in lieu.

The four of us were billeted at a nearby hotel overnight and the following morning we were escorted by the RAF Movements Officer to London Airport where we were booked in with KLM and cleared through baggage, customs and passport control. We discovered that the first part of our flight would be in a Lockheed Convair (a twin-engine, feeder-line aircraft) to Schipol (Amsterdam) airport, where we would transfer to a Lockheed Constellation, a four-engine, long-range aircraft, for the rest of our flight to Cairo, via Rome.

The flight to Schipol was of short duration but even so, KLM demonstrated its passenger handling efficiency and hospitality dispensing welcome refreshment. On landing at Schipol, we disembarked and were taken to the passenger lounge to await the next part of our flight, which was scheduled to take off later that evening. KLM again merited full marks when they provided us with a pre-flight five course meal, plus refreshment. Afterwards, full of food, drink and bonhomie we were unanimous in our opinion that this was definitely the way to take up a posting! From now on they could keep their 'unexploded' (unexpired) portions of the day's rations, which was the usual transit fodder.

At the appointed time we boarded the Constellation and settled in our seats. We had barely got airborne before the KLM hospitality again became evident – the stewardesses circulating among the passengers dispensing refreshments. As it was a night flight we were unable to make out much of the area over which we flew and spent the time either reading or sleeping, with the cabin staff providing nightcaps at regular intervals if you were so inclined!

The flight proceeded as planned and we landed at Rome Airport where we disembarked and had a snack while the aircraft was refuelled. When this was completed we re-boarded and resumed our flight to Cairo where we landed early in the morning.

Even though it was early in the day by the time we had cleared customs we were feeling the effects of the unaccustomed heat – it was the beginning of August, one of the hottest months. RAF movements personnel then escorted us to the railway station where we boarded a train for the Suez Canal Zone. After our most pleasant flight from the UK with KLM, this was quite an anti-climax, what with the heat and the insistence of the Egyptian pedlars attempting to sell us their (mostly pornographic postcard) wares. The train journey from Cairo to the Canal Zone took longer than the flight from the UK to Cairo and we were glad when it was over.

We were then transported to the Reception Depot at El Hamra, here we stayed four days being booked in administratively and medically, to check we hadn't brought any diseases with us!

After all these preliminaries were successfully endured, we were sent to join our Squadrons at RAF Kabrit. One of the navigators of our party Ieun Thomas, and myself went to 114 Squadron. At that time there were five Dakota Squadrons, plus the Middle East Communications Flight based there.

It didn't take me long to get settled in and to visit the Camp Tailor who provided me with some decent fitting KD instead of the knee-covering shorts provided in the interim by stores, which were seemingly designed to prevent you from ever getting your knees brown!

After a flying acceptance check I was put on the Route Flying roster which resulted in my being introduced to flying various scheduled passenger and freight flights allocated to the squadron on a monthly basis. My first flights were supervised to familiarise me with the procedures for flying the routes and the landings and take-offs at the various staging-post airfields.

Our routes were many and varied, Fayid – the main Middle East staging-post, to Malta (Luqa) via El Adem, Benina and Castel-Benito (all familiar places during the Middle East campaign of the Second World War). This schedule was nicknamed the 'egg run' by the crews, because at all the stops the meal provided was invariably egg and chips! Landing and taking-off from some of these airfields could be interesting, especially landing at night, when you were warned by Air Traffic Control to beware of donkeys and camels crossing the runways! It could be quite disconcerting to be committed to landing and see illuminated in the beam of your landing-lights numerous animals ambling across the runway, 'Full throttle, wheels and flaps up, going round again!'

Our other scheduled routes were Fayid to Khormaksar (Aden) and Asmara (Eritrea) both via Wadi-Halfa and Khartoum. Fayid to Eastleigh (Nairobi), via Wadi-Halfa, Khartoum and Juba, Fayid to Habbaniya (Iraq). Fayid to Mafraq and Aqaba (Jordan) and Fayid to Cyprus (Nicosia).

As well as passenger and freight flying we had other commitments such as Army support, carrying out parachute and freight dropping exercises from time to time and special tasks such as providing logistic support for the Lancaster Radar Reconnaissance Squadron and the Fighter Squadrons based in the Canal Zone, when they went on operational detachments. One to Taif (Saudi Arabia) to support the Military Mission based there, was unusual in that we had to carry an Arab guide to make sure we didn't fly over the 'forbidden' cities. Also, the standard breakfast provided at Taif by the Military Mission was usually a bottle of beer! I soon learned when flying on specials that we had to be prepared for every eventuality!

Some of our normal routine mundane passenger and freight trips had their own particular interest, especially those to Asmara and Aqaba. The former Italian airfield was literally perched on top of the mountains and the thought of losing an engine on take-off concentrated one's mind considerably, while Aqaba, at the top of the Gulf of Aqaba, had a natural surface runway of only 800 yards and was located on the Jordan/Israel border, which we weren't allowed to infringe. We were restricted to right-hand circuits and as the hills rose steeply to the right in close proximity to the airfield, take-offs and circuits could be very tricky particularly in cross-wind conditions when you had a heavy load. Short-field take-off procedure was standard practice – max lift flap, taps (throttles) opened to 'full chat' (wide open) with brakes on, then release the brakes and hope you'd reach safety speed and get airborne before you ran out of take-off run! The additional hazard of the close proximity of the hills as you turned right after take-off could make things just a bit hairy, especially in the heat of the day. WAT Limits (Weight, Altitude and Temperature Limitations), to replace this seat of the pants stuff, were in the distant future!

I'm pleased to say that the two instances described above were the exception rather than the rule. The weather conditions for flying were generally very good and some of the sights from the air were unforgettable. Seeing the ruined city of Petra in Jordan for the first time and the 'Juba' herd (hundreds and hundreds of migrating wildebeest) seen while flying on the way to Nairobi, will always live in my memory.

Of course we did get some adverse weather conditions affecting flying on occasion. Dust storms such as the Khamsin and the Simoom when dust rose thousands of feet, limited visibility and penetrated every available aperture. Then during winter we were subject to vigorous low pressure systems (Cyprus Lows) in the eastern Mediterranean on the egg run schedule and the flights to Cyprus which could make things a little difficult, seeing that we had little in the way of navigation and landing aids.

Douglas Dakota.

Vickers Valetta.

For me the flying was always interesting, but there was the odd niggle and disappointment. The first was when our 'Goonie Birds' (Dakotas) were withdrawn in late 1949 and replaced with Vickers Valettas, which in no time at all became known as the 'Pigs'. We converted onto them in the Zone, with instructors sent out from the UK. One pleasant diversion in which I participated during conversion was flying in a formation escort to HM Destroyer *Amethyst* as it proceeded through the Suez Canal on its triumphal return to the UK. Escaping from the Chinese blockade in the Yangste River and running the gauntlet of the Chinese artillery which inflicted damage and casualties, had resulted in her skipper, Commander Kerrans, and other members of the crew receiving decorations for bravery.

After completing our conversion onto Valettas, to compensate for the loss of our favoured Daks, we were given the perk of flying them back to the UK. We were able to spend some leave there before picking up our new Valettas and flying them back to the Zone. I was lucky enough to get back to spend my leave at home over Christmas 1949 and as I was hoping to get my family out to the Zone as soon as I could, it was an opportunity to bring back some household necessities.

After my leave expired early in the New Year I collected a new aircraft from RAF Honington and flew it to RAF Manston to clear customs and to return to Kabrit. However, we were held up at Manston until the en route weather conditions improved. When they did we were informed that instead of flying the usual return route, we were required to fly our first leg to Dijon (France) to deliver spares for the repair of a Ferry Flight Vampire which had damaged its undercarriage and a tip-tank, landing there on its way to Singapore. Our perk was that we were given an 'Imprest' to cover our expenses for a night stop at Dijon. Whacko!

Our flight to the French Air Force fighter airfield at Dijon passed without incident and on landing we were met by the RAF Liaison Officer, who had arranged our transit accommodation and also for us to have our evening meal at an *estaminet* where he obviously had an arrangement. He assured us that he was only looking after our interests then drove us to our hotel and left us to our own devices.

After we'd booked in and cleaned ourselves up we made our way to the *estaminet* where we had some refreshment and a very good meal, during which we were entertained by the resident 'orchestra' – a trio playing some typical French pop music of the day.

During the evening our navigator, a young Canadian sergeant, paid a visit to what he assumed was the gents. When he returned he informed us that it was a 'unisex job'. Apparently as he was performing, a female voice behind him wished him 'Bon soir'. Embarrassed, he turned around to discover a youngish lady seated on the throne with her undergarments around her ankles. He beat a hasty retreat. However, as he was recounting his adventure to us the youngish lady passed our table and gave him a dazzling smile. He put the obvious invitation on hold, but as the evening wore on and more refreshment was consumed I anticipated what might happen. So I lowered the boom and reminded him and the rest of the crew that I was planning an early take-off and to put any intentions of late-night entente cordiale out of their lecherous minds. As you can imagine my popularity plummeted, but my advice prevailed and at the end of the evening I got them all back to the hotel without any of them falling by the wayside.

The following morning we took off and set course for Malta where we landed at Luqa several hours later. After a night stop we resumed and completed our flight to Kabrit staging through Castel-Benito – Benina – El Adem and Fayid.

Although we all suffered from Dakota-itis we got used to flying the pig and even developed what could be described as a love/hate relationship.

It was a military version of the civil Viking, powered by two Hercules 250's of 2,000hp each and could carry thirty-four troops with full equipment or twenty stretcher-cases, or twenty paratroops with 350 lb containers – it also could be used for glider-towing. It had a maximum speed of 258mph at 10,000 feet, a service ceiling of 28,700 feet and a range of 2,648 miles at 239mph – better figures but more difficult handling qualities than the Daks.

Life on the squadron in the Middle East at this time was a pleasant change from the cold and still rationed UK. The Royal Air Force at this time comprised mostly ex-Second World War personnel and Kabrit was no exception. Wing Commander L.V.E Atkinson DSO DFC, an ex-Blenheim ace was OC Flying Wing. He was replaced later by Wing Commander Bill Tacon DSO DFC, an ex-wartime Mosquito pilot. Our 114 Squadron CO was S/Ldr Hugh Everitt DSO DFC, ex-Lancasters (50 Squadron) later relieved by S/Ldr K.V. Gilling, a wartime Lysander pilot. A good proportion of the aircrew on all of the squadrons were also ex-wartime operators, consequently a great sense of camaraderie persisted. Inter-squadron rivalry was evident in most activities – in the air, on the sports fields and in the messes especially on Dining-in Nights, during the after-dinner games. Some of the squadrons had mascots and ours was Wimpey a cross-bred bull-terrier whose minder, Harry Gill, our Navigation Leader, brought him to all dining-in nights – formally dressed of course in stiff white collar and black bow-tie! They were both partial to Stella and suffered the consequent hangovers together!

Service married accommodation was in short supply but approved civilian hirings were available and I managed to get a bungalow situated very near Kabrit on the shore of the Bitter Lake. It had its short comings but these were more than compensated for by its location and the constant good weather, ideal conditions in which our small daughter revelled – in no time she could swim as well as she could walk. These conditions prevailed until the powers that be reached the decision that the transport squadrons should move to Fayid, the main staging post, to obviate the time-wasting and uneconomical system of pre-positioning from Kabrit when carrying out scheduled flights. The fighter squadrons at present occupying Fayid would replace us. I should imagine that flash of genius must have merited CBs, CBEs etc. in the Honours List! The move took place as planned and we reluctantly left Kabrit and took up residence at Fayid, which meant we had further to travel to indulge in our aquatic activities. However you can't win them all.

Throughout history the Middle East has been politically volatile and during my tour there were one or two hiccups. For the first eighteen months that I was in the Zone, things were relatively peaceful, that is except for the never-ending task of protecting our military establishments against the Egyptian loose wallahs who were forever attempting to penetrate camps at night to filch anything they could lay their hands on. Our armed guards patrolled the perimeters and from time to time there was the odd dust-up.

The first major hiccup occurred when Mohammed Mossadegh, the Persian Prime Minister, attacked the Anglo-Iranian Oil Company by passing the Oil Nationalisation Act in 1951. The British Government resented this and prepared to take retaliatory action if they considered it to be necessary.

The transport squadrons based at Fayid were heavily involved in these contingency measures, their task being to fly stores (arms and ammunition) at night to Kuwait and Shaibah. We would fly to Deversoir near Ismalia, load up with stores and set course across the Sinai Desert to the Gulf of Aqaba, then turn onto course for either Kuwait or Shaibah as required. It wasn't long before we were out of range of any navigational aid, so we had to rely on DR and Astro and hope our navigator was on the ball. However flogging across the Arabian desert at night could have its compensations as it was relatively cool and the night sky with its myriad stars couldn't fail to arouse a feeling of wonderment in the mind of the most confirmed cynic. But, come the dawn, the inevitable question from the navigator was 'Can anyone see the pipeline?' Meaning the oil pipeline which runs across the desert to the Mediterranean. If you were lucky and saw it you could then follow it and map-read to your destination, if not you carried on flying until you reached the Persian Gulf, verified a pinpoint and back-tracked to your destination.

Shaibah – its 'blues' song was famous throughout the RAF at that time and featured in most sing-songs during stag parties. It was also one of the hottest places in that part of the Middle East and was not the place in which to hang about, so after landing in the early morning, the drill was to offload as quickly as possible, refuel, have a quick snack and get airborne before the temperature started going off the clock. On one trip however, I was caught out. As I was doing my pre-landing check, I called to the signaller to check the level of hydraulic oil in the reservoir located near his position. To my dismay he reported that no fluid was showing in the observation window, indicating a possible leak. So to avoid having to carry out a possible wheels-up landing, I selected my landing-gear down immediately, hoping I could use residual oil which might still be in the pipe-lines. I was lucky, I got the U/C down and locked and was able to carry out a safe landing.

On examination it was found that the hydraulic pump had seized up and would have to be replaced. Again I was fortunate, a new pump was available and the ground crew got cracking. I didn't envy them their task as by that time the temperature was rising rapidly. We were more fortunate. We were able to enjoy the comparative coolness in the Transit Mess but by the time our aircraft was declared serviceable it was midday and the temperature was well over a hundred. I had no desire to spend a night at Shaibah, so I made preparations to get off as soon as possible.

My outside check was one of the quickest I've ever done. The aircraft skin was too hot to touch and by the time I'd climbed aboard, the light blue flying overalls I was wearing were a sodden navy-blue. I took off as soon as I could and didn't hang about on the return flight. I had another priority for getting back because in July 1951 our second daughter had been born, so with a new baby and a three-year old daughter, it was all hands to the pumps at home!

While the dispute concerning the nationalisation of the oil in Persia was being sorted out politically we were beset with another more serious problem. In September 1951, Egypt abrogated the Suez Canal Peace Treaty of 1936 – anti-British rioting broke out in towns in the Zone and the situation quickly deteriorated. The families of some servicemen were molested and there were cases of looting. We flew Army reinforcements into the Zone and the wives and families of servicemen (mine among them) were evacuated back to the UK. Situations such as this serve as a timely reminder to we servicemen and our country, of the debt of gratitude we owe to wives and families who follow and support their service husbands unselfishly in peace and war, regardless of the discomfort and danger it entails.

All the squadrons were put on an emergency footing, all living-out personnel were recalled to their bases and personal arms were issued. The Egyptian civilian workers employed at bases all left and we had to look after ourselves. The commodities previously supplied by the Egyptians such as fresh vegetables and Stella (tragically!) were unavailable so we had to use alternative sources. We also had to do our own dhobi (laundry). Additional flights were scheduled for the Transport Squadrons, to Mafraq (Jordan) to bring in vegetables and to Nicosia for eggs and fruit. We used the facilities available to other staging posts to replace our liquid shortages – Saccone and Speed of Malta did a roaring trade!

The political situation deteriorated further when armed Egyptian police in their barracks at Ismalia refused to submit to British authority and opened fire an our troops. Our troops retaliated resulting in forty-six of the policemen being killed. No casualties were suffered by our forces.

In the meantime the Egyptian Army sent a heavily armed force into the Zone from Egypt. It got within eleven miles of Fayid before turning back as a result of being repeatedly buzzed by our fighters. Our involvement in the action was to airlift the paratroop reinforcements from Nicosia to the Zone who took over complete control of all the key points on the canal.

We transport squadrons continued to fulfil our normal route commitments as well as the extra cabbage and fruit runs, despite the difficulties of being under siege. The terrorist activity in the Zone also required a 'Casevac' contingency to deal with any emergency to fly in casualties which occurred from time to time in the outlying areas, to the Fayid Central Hospital.

This uneasy situation continued through to the end of 1951, when I was reaching the end of my tour. At the end of January 1952, on return from a scheduled trip to Cyprus I was informed that I was now 'tour expired' and that if I got my skates on, was cleared and got myself down to Fanara on the Bitter Lakes by the following morning, I could take over as OC RAF Troops on a requisitioned passenger liner returning from Malaya to the UK.

It was no contest. I cleared Fayid, packed my kit in anything available, such as kit-bags and Cyprus fruit baskets, got to Fanara and boarded the liner with time to spare. Once aboard I discovered that my troops comprised a few airmen and their families being evacuated back to the UK.

I reported to the captain, who informed me that it would be part of my duty to accompany him or one of his officers on daily inspections to ensure that my RAF contingent didn't make a mess of his nice clean ship. Apparently, they had just got it back to being shipshape and Bristol fashion after transporting Fijian troops from Fiji to Malaya to join the forces combating the Communist forces there. During their voyage the barefoot troops were introduced to wearing boots and to break them in they were marched round and round the decks. The Major in charge of them commented wryly that he didn't realise before he left Fiji that they were going to have to walk to Malaya!

During our conversations after 'rounds' I discovered that the captain had lost a son who was killed while flying with Bomber Command during the Second World War. That probably accounted for the fatherly interest he took in the RAF contingent throughout the voyage, especially when we ran into a spot of heavy weather as we sailed through the Bay of Biscay.

We were all glad to get back to dear old Blighty, but our arrival was tinged with sadness, when we learnt that His Majesty King George VI had died. Before proceeding on my disembarkation leave to rejoin my family I had to report to Air Ministry to get my next posting and while there I was able to witness the cortege conveying His late Majesty proceeding on its way to Westminster where he would lie in state – a sad occasion.

When I had my interview with Postings I discovered that W/Cdr Bill Tacon, OC Flying Wing Fayid had recommended I be posted to the RAF Central Flying School after my leave. I was going back to school to be trained as a Flying Instructor, a posting I hadn't anticipated but on reflection realised was a step in the right direction.

No. 114 Squadron, RAF, Fayid, 1951.

HMS Amethyst *in Suez Canal.*

Valettas escorting HMS Amethyst *through the Suez Canal.*

Fifteen
To Learn and Teach

When my disembarkation leave ended, I reported to RAF South Cerney to commence the Flying Instructors' course. I found the course was conducted in two phases, the initial part at South Cerney followed by the second at RAF Little Rissington, home of CFS (the RAF Central Flying Instructors School).

Before commencing the first phase we were given a short flying refresher course on Harvards. It was a nice change for me after flying heavy twins for the past two and a half years – it was a long time since I'd been upside-down!

After the short Harvard session we went to RAF Pembrey on a Leadership Course, where we lived under canvas, did our own cooking, and were given other tasks to stimulate our self-reliance and leadership qualities under stress. It also honed our sense of humour, an essential requirement for any would-be flying instructor. This latter characteristic was really tested to the full when it came to having to put up with the amateur cooking, because none of us was in the cordon bleu class. However, we survived that and the rest of the leadership course then returned to South Cerney where we started the course proper and were introduced to the aspects of instructional technique both on the ground and in the air.

The airborne part of our training was in the Percival Prentice, a single-engine low-wing monoplane in which we were taught to fly and synchronise our instructional patter, a function that required undivided concentration. After each dual exercise we were sent off with fellow students to practice mutually. Our programme included the technique of teaching all aspects of flying from basic to the advanced phases. When we got to the aerobatics stage I found initially that my patter had a tendency to dry-up when I was upside-down. However, I improved with practice.

After completing the day flying schedule of exercises we progressed to the night flying phase. One of the exercises listed on the night flying programme was Precision Flying and we were all curious to discover what this entailed. We were enlightened during our last night flying detail. My instructor for this exercise was Flt Lt Ian Pedder (later Air Marshal, Sir Ian Pedder KCB OBE DFC) who was also a member of the South Cerney Formation Aerobatic Team. They carried out their formation flying with their aircraft tied together! We all admired their skill but were of the opinion they were slightly 'harpic' (clean round the bend)!

When we got airborne he told me to climb the aircraft up to 5,000 feet and level off. Although it was very dark it was quite clear and when I levelled off I was able to pinpoint our position with the aid of the lights of Cirencester. After I'd done so and retrimmed, he

Percival Prentice.

told me to do a roll! I couldn't believe I'd heard correctly but when he repeated it, I thought 'oh dear, the poor so-and-so has lost his marbles.' I said, 'You're not serious, are you?' His reaction was to take control and roll the aircraft to the right, then hand over control to me, saying, 'Go on, there's nothing to it, give it a go.' So if only to attempt to disguise the fact I was chicken, I lined up on a well-lit road leading out of Cirencester and went through the motions – we didn't fall out of the sky, but I'm sure it was more by good luck than good management. We spent the rest of the detail mostly upside-down and to be honest by the end of it I was enjoying myself – maybe going round the bend is catching! When we landed I was cautioned not to make this CFS interpretation of Precision Flying public and also not make night aerobatics a part of my instructional repertoire if I managed to graduate – as if I would!

When I completed the South Cerney phase I then proceeded to RAF Little Rissington for the remainder of the course. At that time I had no experience on jets so I joined the piston engine Harvard Flight. I looked forward to flying it again. My previous experience had made me conversant with most of its essential characteristics, especially its inherent tendency to ground-loop during landings in cross-wind conditions. This stood me in good stead when flying mutual details especially if my partner taking the part of the pupil called, 'You have control', when he realised he was making a cock-up of a landing and handed over at the final stage.

As I've mentioned, up to this time I had no experience of flying jets. However, the CFS powers that be apparently thought this omission should be rectified, so they decided that U/T piston-engine instructors should be given the opportunity to fly a Vampire they just happened to have available.

This Vampire turned out to be a Mk V single-seat fighter/bomber version, so no dual flying was possible and our conversion took the form of reading the Pilots' Notes while sitting in the cockpit to familiarise ourselves with the controls and instrument layout under the supervision of a jet qualified instructor. This included having the twin fuselage booms pulled down to ground level to demonstrate the angle of attack (flight attitude) not to assume when coming into land.

So when my turn came there I was sitting in the cockpit when said jet instructor invited me to light the fire (start the engine). Following the instructions outlined in Pilots' Notes, I did as bid. When the Goblin flamed into life, my excitement rose well above the TGT (Turbine Gas Temperature) but when the instructor patted me on the head and said nonchalantly, 'OK, off you go', it nearly went right off the clock! Before I could enter into any form of negotiation, he was organising the ground crew to prepare to pull the chocks away! Hadn't he heard of human rights?

I reluctantly called Air Traffic Control on the R/T, blurting out the intentions my jet 'sponsor' had conned me into and asked for permission to taxi. They happily granted my request, supplying all the information I would require – runway in use, barometric pressure-setting, wind velocity and weather details etc. Accepting the inevitable, I made sure that my bible (Pilots' Notes) was handy, carried out my pre-taxi check, then hoping I had omitted nothing, I waved 'chocks away'. Taxiing from dispersal I gave my sponsor a half-hearted thumbs up. I may be wrong but I think I saw him out of the corner of my eye look up and clasp his hands in supplication!

This was not only my first jet sortie but the first time I'd handled an aircraft with a nose-wheel under-carriage configuration. I was pleasantly surprised to discover that taxiing was much easier compared with the tail-wheel types I was used to. Also as the Vampire was a relatively small aircraft with a short undercarriage (the overall height to the top of the canopy was only seven feet) I got the impression I was perched on a tall bike!

Arriving at the take-off point without mishap, I carried out the checks and asked for

De Havilland Vampire Mark V FB.

take-off clearance. Air Traffic gave me the OK, so I turned onto the runway centre-line and after a quick check of the temperatures, pressures and instruments to make sure everything was working properly I opened up the throttle. I must have been a little impetuous, because something (the Vampire) hit me in the middle of the spine, forcing me back in my seat. It streaked down the runway while I attempted to collect my scattered wits and catch up with the little beast! Before I knew it I was airborne, the aircraft having got there without much assistance from me. I think I was passing through 200 feet before I got the undercarriage retracted – let's face it my reactions were still in the pre-jet category. Another shock, a quick glance at the ASI (Airspeed Indicator) told me I was climbing faster than we'd ever achieved in a screaming dive in our bombers at the beginning of the Second World War!

As the Vampire continued heavenwards like a homesick angel, I realised (to use a royal epithet) that I would have to get my bloody finger out, but quick! Stiffening my upper lip in the approved British fashion, I took a firm grip on myself and consulted Pilots' Notes while choking back the urge to yell, 'mayday, mayday, mayday' on the VHF Emergency Frequency.

Reading avidly, I managed to get things sorted out to trim the aircraft in a steady climb at the recommended airspeed and engine settings. Having achieved that, I tackled my next problem, where on earth had I got to since getting airborne – in navigation parlance I was uncertain of my position (also known as lost). However you can't keep a good man down. I levelled off, fished out of my flying overalls pocket a map of the local area and after doing a bit of mental back-track navigation I had a rough idea where I was. Shortly afterwards I was able to get a pinpoint and confirm my position.

Next on the agenda, how to get to know how to fly this De Havilland demon before I would have to answer the sixty-four thousand dollar question, 'How do I get it back on terra firma in one piece?' Out came the bible again and following the instructions (to the letter I might add) I climbed to 8,000 feet and carried out a bit of general handling, turns, climbs, dives etc., slow flying and lowering the undercarriage and flaps. Having done that and having convinced myself I could now hack it, I thought I'd better get back to base before my fuel ran out. Not trusting my navigation, I called the ranch (base) for a steer (course back to base). They obliged and it wasn't long before I joined the circuit and using the 'know how' from my high level practice I was able to get the Vampire down on the deck in one piece. I cleared the runway, uncrossed my fingers, heaved a sigh of relief, taxied back to dispersal and shut down.

My sponsor was waiting for me and as I unstrapped and climbed out of the cockpit, he asked, 'Any problems?' Lying through my teeth, I replied, 'No, nothing to it.' 'Oh, good!' he said, 'How would you like to have it refuelled and take it up again?' Forgetting the old Service maxim, 'Keep your mouth shut, your bowel open, but DON'T volunteer', that had been drummed into me at an early age, I meekly accepted his offer. So, being lumbered I again stuck my nose into the book of words.

By the time the Vampire was refuelled, I had regained some of my composure and having survived my initial flight as a reluctant jet jockey I was convincing myself there was nothing to it and that I had everything under control. I even kidded myself that with a bit more practice, I might even become a 'steely-eyed' fighter boy. To further the illusion, I called nonchalantly to the ground crew in the best Hollywood fighter pilot style, 'OK, let's go, kick the tyre, light the fire, kindle my flame, I'm hot to trot.' I don't think I impressed anybody.

After doing the outside checks, I again climbed aboard and strapped in. It wasn't long before I was taxiing out for another dice in the wide blue yonder. When I obtained take-off clearance, having previously learnt my lesson, I was ready for and savoured the kick that I got when I opened the throttle. The Vampire streaked down the runway, and I eased it into the air, retracted the undercarriage and trimmed it into the climb – this is the life – jet flying – a piece of cake!

It was a beautiful day, only a few cumulus clouds in an azure sky. I levelled off at 15,000 feet and headed for the designated aerobatic area – now where else would a jet 'ace' (with all of one hour's jet experience) head for! Arriving in the area I had another browse through Pilots' Notes to verify the recommended speeds for the various aerobatic manoeuvres. I then spent another few minutes urging myself to get on with it. Eventually I tried a barrel-roll to the right (my best side). When I recovered, although I wasn't heading in the precise direction I'd planned, I thought it wasn't bad for a first attempt. With my confidence growing all the time I tried another two, one left and one right and even if they weren't spot on I thought they weren't bad for a beginner. I then tried a couple of slow rolls and loops, however during one of the loops I must have pulled it a little too tight, which caused me to 'grey out'. After that salutary reminder not to push my luck, I flew straight and level until my sphincter stopped 'twittering' and trying to bite lumps out of my parachute!

A check of my fuel gauges told me it was go home time, so I headed back to base on a gentle let-down and informed Air Traffic Control. I was given permission to join the circuit but advised there was a cross-wind affecting landings on the runway in use. That didn't bother me – jet flying – a simple game – I'll show 'em how it should be done! Joining the circuit downwind, I then turned onto finals, nicely crabbing to compensate for the drift. However, as I came over the end of the runway, preparing to kick the aircraft straight, round out and execute the perfect landing, a gust of wind caught the aircraft and the so-and-so runway gremlins lowered the surface by at least six feet. The Vampire thumped in and cavorted down the runway in a series of hiccups. I got no sympathy from Air Traffic Control as I endeavoured to control the aircraft and the situation. The Duty Controller, who obviously had aspirations of becoming resident comedian at the London Palladium, advised me to 'bounce left at the next intersection' – cheeky sod. Eventually I got everything sorted out and taxied back to dispersal, reflecting that Sir Frank Whittle had a lot to answer for! A very chastened 'jet ace' shut down the Vampire and sidled back to the crew-room where a few of my fellow students who had witnessed my performance were only too willing to offer their commiseration and advice. So much for my first sorties into the jet age!

I resumed my training on the Harvard and progressed favourably through the stages to my final check which resulted in me being awarded my certificate from the Commandant of the RAF Central Flying Instructors' School, confirming that I was now a fully qualified Flying Instructor (Pistons).

Shortly afterwards I was also given the good news that I had been granted a 'Branch' Permanent Commission, which now meant I could remain on flying duties until a retirement age of fifty-five depending on my retaining a full flying medical standard. My promotion prospects would be restricted, but I was quite willing to accept this because I had no ambitions to become Chief of the Air Staff. All I wanted was to continue flying as long as I could.

After graduation I was posted to instruct on twin-engine Airspeed Oxfords at an AFTS (Advanced Flying Training School) at RAF Pershore in Worcestershire. Once again I thought my superiors were being slightly perverse, training me to instruct on singles then sending me to instruct on twins. However mine was not to reason why. I suppose their thinking was that after absorbing the CFS instructing technique, one should have the know-how to instruct on anything. Luckily as I'd flown Oxfords previously I was able to adapt and commence 'earning my corn' without much delay.

At this time in 1952 the students at Pershore were for the most part specially selected National Servicemen, who had applied to do their stint in the Services as U/T pilots. Having made it through their EFTS (Elementary Flying Training School) they were now going through the advanced stage before getting their wings. Each Flying Instructor was allocated four students, flying with two in the morning and two in the afternoon, to fit in with the well tried training procedure of alternating flying and ground instruction. As can be imagined the flying commitment was somewhat hectic at the beginning of each course until the students got to the solo stage, each instructor doing up to eight hours instructional flying per day. However, the job satisfaction of being able to send a pupil solo, was well worth the effort and I recall my pleasure when I sent my students solo for the first time.

There were some disappointments when despite all efforts it became obvious that a student was experiencing difficulty. In such cases sometimes a change of instructor solved the problem. If this didn't do the trick he was passed to the Squadron Commander for a

North American Harvard.

check ride. If he failed to make it he then flew with the Chief Instructor who would decide whether to persevere with extra instruction or to initiate the chop (cessation of training), a dreadful fate to endure.

I experienced a great deal of pleasure helping and guiding students through the various stages of the course, from getting them to their first day solo then to the more advanced aspects such as pilot navigation, instrument flying and night flying.

Most instructors had secondary duty tasks other than flying. Mine being the responsibility for lecturing and training the students in 'Escape and Evasion' and 'Resistance to Interrogation Techniques'. During my wartime operational career as a necessity I had taken great interest in the subject. Fortunately I wasn't called upon to use the knowledge I acquired, but realised the importance of it should the need have arisen, especially having spoken with quite a few of my squadron contemporaries after the war who had been shot down and spent years in the bag. Our Chief Instructor, Wing Commander Pat Sands was also an enthusiast and decreed that all students after receiving instruction in escape and evasion and interrogation technique would participate in at least one escape and evasion exercise during their course.

The responsibility for organising all aspects of these exercises fell on me. This entailed selection of an exercise area, liaison with local landowners to get permission for the evaders and defence forces to traverse their land, the setting up of safe houses for a resistance network (fellow flying instructors) an interrogation team (co-opted Intelligence Officers) and a Stalag in which to incarcerate captured evaders. The defence forces who co-operated wholeheartedly, comprised the Worcestershire County and City Police, plus personnel of a training battalion from the locally based REME Unit (Royal Electrical and Mechanical Engineers).

Each exercise lasted three days, generally over a weekend, and was usually carried out with enthusiasm from all concerned. Even the student evaders who had to walk/run for miles while being harried by the defence forces, sleep rough, and endure interrogation and incarceration if they were captured affirmed they got some fun out of it. There were numerous stories of their exploits. One crew of evaders who had managed to contact the resistance network were being ferried in a rubber dinghy across the river unfortunately they lost their paddles and were swept down river. Luckily they managed to scramble ashore and take refuge in the crypt of Worcester Cathedral, where they spent a wet and uncomfortable night before being apprehended by the City Police. They had been alerted by a verger who suspected the Cathedral was being burgled. The City Police also had their share of tribulation when an over-keen member of the resistance immobilised their headquarters for some time by lobbing a smoke bomb into the City Police Station. They were not amused, and the outcome was that for future exercises the use of smoke bombs was forbidden. There was also the case of one of the senior RAF staff who decided to give an example by being an evader, got himself captured, interrogated and thrown in the Stalag. After spending an uncomfortable night, he pulled rank and returned to his quarters, but not for long. An even more senior member of staff was very amused to learn of his capture, but when he learned of his subsequent action, went to his quarters and convinced him it would better if he returned to the Stalag and gave a good example to the student captives. He reluctantly agreed!

In addition to giving the students flying instruction on Oxfords, we also added a little spice to the course by taking them flying in the single-engine tandem-seater De Havilland Chipmunk (a delightful little aircraft) from time to time, re-introducing them to aerobatics and low flying.

Our designated low-flying area was between Tewkesbury and the Malvern Hills and crossing the river south of Tewkesbury bridge there was a power-line. Flying under it was a challenge no red-blooded aviator could resist and few of us did!

After instructing students for about eighteen months I was transferred within the unit to instruct with the newly-formed Refresher Flight, which had been formed for the purpose of justifying flying-pay bonus, by re-introducing pilots back on flying who had spent a lot of time in Staff jobs. Some of them hadn't flown for some considerable time, for instance my first student hadn't flown an aircraft with a retractable undercarriage! The next one's last sortie had been in a Leigh-light Wellington during the Second World War – it was now 1953.

About this time the Ministry of Defence decided, because of cuts in the Defence budget, to close down a certain number of flying schools and unfortunately our AFTS was one of them, which resulted in a certain amount of redundancy among the flying instructors. I was unfortunately one of them.

The Postings Staff at Flying Training Command Headquarters had the unenviable task of trying to accommodate us. We were all hoping to be posted to another flying unit, but when my case came up for review, it was brought to my attention it was about time I did a ground tour, as I had been on flying duties continuously since the beginning of the war. So I had no choice but to reluctantly accept their decision.

Consequently I was posted to Air Ministry on an Air Intelligence Course. It turned out to be one of the most interesting courses I experienced during my career.

Sixteen
'V' Bomber Force

After successfully completing the Air Intelligence course at Air Ministry I was posted to be Intelligence/Operations Officer at RAF Gaydon in Warwickshire. Gaydon had been selected as the location for the OCU (Operational Conversion Unit) for the UK Independent Nuclear Deterrent, 'V' Bomber Force, eventually comprising the four-jet Valiants, Victors and Vulcans, I went there in March 1954 as one of the advance party. Gaydon was originally a wartime PR (Photographic Reconnaissance) and bomber airfield, but to accommodate the new four-jet 'V' bomber requirements, it had been transformed. Two new hangars of massive proportions had been constructed as well as a new NATO type runway (3,300 yards long) with a parallel perimeter track, plus a new special bomb dump and a flight simulator building. New operational, technical and administration blocks had also been built. A new domestic site comprising Sick Quarters, Messes, Stores and Personnel accommodation was on the site of the old airfield runways, consequently until they were narrowed, Gaydon had the widest roads of any Station in the RAF.

Our task as the advance party was to prepare for the influx of the main body of personnel and equipment, which included the new Vickers 'Valiant' four-jet bomber, the first of the 'V' Bomber aircraft. Until a permanent Police Security Officer was posted in I was also responsible for security and temporarily I/C RAF Police.

Personnel who would have access to highly classified nuclear information were subjected to a new special security clearance (positive vetting) irrespective of rank. I had been put through the positive vetting mill when I was selected for the Intelligence Officer post, and now it was my responsibility to initiate the clearance of designated personnel as and when they were posted in.

While we waited for the arrival of the Valiants, more personnel were posted in and the various sections took shape and were brought up to strength. They included the nucleus of the specially selected flying and ground instructional staff who had gone through the various aircraft industry makers courses. Most aircrew were experienced ex-Canberra fliers. The OC Flying Wing, Wing Commander Lewis Hodges (later Air Chief Marshal Sir Lewis Hodges KCB CBE DSO★ DFC★) had recently been involved with the Bomber Command participation in the UK – Australia air race. The first aircraft we got on our inventory was not a Valiant but an Airspeed Oxford for use by the Station Commander Group Captain B.K. Burnett DFC AFC BA (later Air Marshal Sir Brian Burnett KCB DFC AFC BA) and the OCU staff. So as an Oxford QFI I was in there, 'like Flynn', because there was nothing in my terms of reference precluding me from flying, even if I was supposed to be on a ground tour. Besides I had to keep my hand in and if I could you can bet I would fly as often as possible – I became the unofficial flying taxi-driver for RAF Gaydon.

My enthusiasm for flying wasn't allowed to affect or hinder my Intelligence duties and I lost no time in organising an Intelligence Library, where aircrew could come and keep themselves up to date with the latest information on Russian aircraft and tactics, this being 1954, the time of the Cold War. With the aid of a kettle, coffee etc., the Intelligence Library became a popular venue for the aircrew who continued to wait for the arrival of their Valiants.

It was during this interim period, that I was 'volunteered' (press-ganged) into accepting an invitation from Bomber Command Headquarters to be one of four RAF aircrew officers to go to Bad Tolz, Germany, to participate in a Survival Escape and Evasion Course and Exercise as guests of the USAF Forces in Europe. This particular course had acquired the reputation, through the grapevine, of being rather strenuous, so for two weeks before I was due to go I did a bit of preparation, walking miles across country, mostly at night, evading the attentions of farm dogs and the local police who were sometimes informed about a suspicious character prowling about the district.

On the appointed day I travelled by train to Harwich where I reported to the Service Movements Centre and met up with the three other RAF aircrew officers from Bomber Command Units who had also been 'volunteered' to participate at Bad Tolz.

We boarded the ferry and sailed to the Hook of Holland, where we disembarked. After clearing customs we took the train to Cologne, where we had to change trains. While waiting

Valiant crew prepare for flight.

Vickers Valiant.

we had the opportunity to leave the station and see some of the city. Although it was now some eight years after the end of the war, most of Cologne was still in ruins, but one of the amazing sights was the huge cathedral, standing practically untouched amid the devastation. Continuous building reconstruction was taking place, even at night under floodlights.

That evening we boarded the night train, the Hook of Holland to Vienna express via Munich, which was our final destination. The night sleeper journey was quite pleasant and we arrived at about seven o'clock in the morning. We disembarked and were informed that USAF transport would take us to Bad Tolz. While waiting we got into conversation with a USAF Tactical Reconnaissance pilot, who was also reporting to the Survival School. Being stationed at a USAF base in the American sector of Germany he was able to provide us with information about the course and the local area. What he told us confirmed what we were about to undergo was certainly no picnic.

Transport finally appeared and we were taken to the Kasserne (barracks) at Bad Tolz where we booked in and were allocated our sparsely furnished rooms. After depositing our kit we were then given the course schedule and issued with American style survival boots – they considered that our 1952 pattern flying/escape boots were inadequate – what had we got into! However the current RAF issue Canberra flying-kit (two-piece outer overalls, long-johns, heavy roll-neck sweaters etc.) we had brought, was considered suitable.

We were advised there was a total of sixty-four officers (sixty USAF and we four RAF) on the course and we were divided into five syndicates. The RAF party would be together in the same section. The proposed 'schedule was daunting and we were advised to have an early night.

The following morning we were roused at 06.30 hours, assembled and taken at the double to the physical training area, where we were subjected to thirty minutes of what they laughingly described as a few loosening-up exercises, such as press-ups etc. We then doubled back to the Kasserne where we carried out our ablutions and policed (cleaned up) our rooms before going to the mess hall for breakfast.

After breakfast it was off to the classrooms, to be instructed in the finer points of survival, escape and evasion and resistance to interrogation. The lectures and demonstrations continued throughout the day (with short breaks for meals) until 21.00 hours. The rest of the day was our own!

This gruelling regime continued for five days, including a session at the parachute-jumping section, where we had to jump from a thirty-four feet high tower in a parachute harness. The harness was attached to a pulley on a cable angled from the tower to a landing sandpit. The abrupt jerk at the end of the harness when you jumped simulated a real drop to perfection, especially when the harness grabbed into your crotch!

On the sixth day we marched to the Tactical Training area where we were shown how to construct para-tepees out of parachute silk, and make gill-nets out of parachute cords. The highlight was a demonstration on how to kill, skin and dress an unfortunate calf, which was then jointed and shared between the syndicates – this took place just before our 'K rations' lunch!

After we had eaten we were taken to a trout farm where we had to fish out a couple of trout each, then to a rabbit compound where we had to catch, kill and gut a rabbit. While this mayhem was going on, little did we suspect that our victims were to be a major part of our food ration for the rest of the exercise. To round off the afternoon we were given the joints of the calf which had been butchered earlier. We cut off strips and put them into a smoke tepee made of parachute silk and branches and smoke dried them into 'jerky', The remains of the joint were cooked in an earth oven (heated stones) and consumed that evening. Later we were taken on a night march to practice map reading and compass handling. This took us into the early hours of the next morning.

We were roused after a few hours sleep to prepare for the actual escape and evasion exercise part of the course. This included building one-man shelters, constructing a pack out of parachute silk to contain our kit – a sleeping bag, a minimum of spare clothing (one pair of socks!) and our rations for the next five days comprising strips of 'jerky', our rabbits and trout we had cooked and a few assorted vegetables, mostly cabbage, potatoes and beetroot.

After breaking camp, pulling down and stowing the tepee materials and 'policing' the area, which meant burning all garbage and filling in the earth latrines, we were ready.

We were told that each syndicate would be transported in trucks to a dropping area from where we had to make our way to a 'safe house' by 06.00 hours the following morning. For safety and security reasons we were advised to travel in pairs. The forces looking to apprehend us an hour after we'd been dropped, comprised American Army and USAF personnel using four-wheel drive jeeps, and the German Civilian Police, some with tracker dogs – how lucky can you get! If – and I suppose our opposition fervently hoped it was a big 'if' – we successfully reached the safe house in the given time, we would be free until briefing for the next phase. Those captured would be 'tenderly' taken care of in the Kasserne dungeons at Bad Tolz and subjected to the niceties – or the finer points – of interrogation until the end of the exercise. The briefing was followed by a short non-denominational religious service. That really cheered us up – did they expect us not to survive? Final preparations included a body search to ensure that we weren't carrying any money to bribe the natives, or to maybe hire a taxi – nor any supplementary rations (chocolate bars etc).

At the appointed time we piled into our trucks – the game was on!

During the course I had struck up a friendship with Captain 'Dutch' Holland, the Tactical Reconnaissance pilot we had met on our arrival. We were in the same syndicate so we agreed to pair off together while we were on the run. During our truck journey we made our plans. The topography on our maps indicated we would have to make our way through thick forests and over cultivated agricultural land, but despite this we decided we'd keep away from the roads and head across country as soon as we left the truck. As the light was fading rapidly, we reckoned the best plan was to go in single file, the one in front choosing the track, while the other kept us on a compass course from behind. We were equipped with shaded hand torches, which we could use surreptitiously to aid our map reading, whenever we felt certain none of the 'enemy' was in the vicinity.

As soon as we were dropped from the truck, we left the road and set off across the Bavarian countryside. We soon discovered the farmers in that area used natural fertiliser (manure) which they scattered liberally on their fields. When you're on the run to avoid being seen, if you detect anyone in the vicinity you hit the deck, so in no time my American oppo and myself were not smelling like roses. At least we thought it might put the dogs off! The distance we had to cover to reach the safe house on the first night was reasonable, in the region of seven or eight miles in a straight line, but with diversions to avoid the searchers, it was further. It must have been beginners' luck or maybe the Defence forces hadn't got into their stride, but we managed to reach our target, a ruined cottage by a stream manned by two of the Directing Staff, and book in before the allotted time expired. They informed us that already some evaders had been captured.

After building our one-man shelters, we thankfully climbed into our sleeping bags and got our heads down. I needed no rocking. When we awoke a few hours later, after a 'marine bath' (a quick wipe all over with a damp face cloth) we built a fire and cooked a meal, a stew from our rations. The beetroot gave it an alarming red colour and it was nothing like your mother used to make but when you're hungry you'll eat anything. After our meal we relaxed until briefing for the next stage.

This procedure continued for the next three days and nights, only the distances to cover increased, the terrain got more difficult and the 'enemy' more determined to capture us. My American partner and myself had evolved a technique which we adopted whenever we were 'jumped'; we split up and shot off in different directions for cover, hid and if we escaped capture, got together again when the coast was clear. We found that walking through the thick forests at night could be difficult because of the limited visibility, but we managed by walking in single file, the leader feeling his way with his home-made walking staff in one hand, pushing aside the branches, while holding onto the rear member's staff with the other hand. The back marker using the compass and map to keep us on track. Even in the forests we had to contend with the 'enemy' who drove up and down the rides attempting to flush us out, but despite their efforts we survived and got through to the last and most difficult stage.

When we were briefed we discovered that the distance we had to cover was comparatively short, but we were also informed that the 'enemy' would be concentrating most of his forces in the vicinity of the final safe house, thus making it even more difficult for us to get through. The safe house was a large tent in a clearing at the top of a hill in a forest.

Dutch and I decided that for this last stage we would split up when we got near the hill where our target was located. Everything went as planned and we reached the parting of the ways without being apprehended, despite having to dodge the patrols from time to time. At the bottom of the hill we wished each other good luck and went our separate ways. I decided to lie up to weigh up the defences and work out how the patrols were operating. I gathered that some seemed to be spiralling the hill from top to bottom, while others swept the area up and down.

When I was sure there were no patrols in the immediate area I set off. The distance to the top of the hill must have been about half a mile, but as we'd been warned at briefing the defences included trip-wire operated thunder-flashes, I took my time, sometimes crawling on all fours, holding a twig in front to help me detect any trip-wires which might be in my path. I made slow but successful progress, but on one occasion I thought I'd had it as a sweep patrol passed within yards of me. I 'froze' beside a fallen tree. One of the patrol actually shone his torch across me, but I kept completely still and remained undiscovered, confirming the theory our Evasion Instructors expounded that in most cases it is movement that leads to discovery. Shortly afterwards the silence was broken by triumphant shouts from the patrol as it flushed out and captured another unfortunate evader in the vicinity. I hoped it wasn't Dutch, my American partner.

After this fortunate escape, and when the patrol had passed from my area I set off again and eventually reached the edge of the clearing where the safe house was located. The large tent was brilliantly lit with pressure lamps. Inside some of the Directing Staff were drinking hot coffee and sadistically inviting evaders to come and join them, obviously hoping they would reveal their position to the patrols and be caught. When I got within a hundred yards of the tent, I heard a patrol coming up behind me, so throwing caution to the winds I got to my feet and took off, covering the distance like the American Olympic sprinter Jesse Owens. As soon as I got near the tent I launched myself through the flap – I'd made it!

After booking in I was given a very welcome cup of coffee, then escorted by a member of the Directing Staff, with three other successful evaders to the nearby road where we boarded transport which took us back to the Kasserne at Bad Tolz where we were allowed to go to our living quarters. I've never luxuriated in a hot shower as I did that morning, or appreciated being able to don clean clothing afterwards. I think I must have stunk like a polecat before I got rid of my grimy, mud-caked flying kit and the accumulated body odour of the past days on the run. Once cleaned up and presentable I went to the mess hall where I consumed a magnificent breakfast, after which I was allowed to return to our quarters and sleep for the rest of the day.

The following morning after breakfast we all assembled in one of the main lecture rooms where we were given the results of the exercise including the tally of successful evaders. Out of the sixty-four participants sixteen had completed all the stages of the exercise without being captured. I was pleased to be one of them, but I was disappointed to learn that my American partner had failed to make the final 'safe house'. He was still on the run when the exercise ended.

We were then taken to another part of the Kasserne, which simulated a Russian

Interrogation Centre. On a brilliantly lit stage, Interrogators in Russian uniform gave a demonstration, using as their victims, two evaders who had been captured at the beginning of the exercise and softened up until now in the Kasserne dungeons. We were seated some way back in complete darkness, invisible to any of the participants on the stage. The demonstration was most efficient and impressive. Afterwards I spoke to one of the two evaders who had been used as guinea-pigs and he told me of his treatment in the Kasserne dungeons after he'd been caught. He told me he was kept in total darkness, with the temperature in his cell varying from freezing cold to unbearable heat, interrupted sleep, constant interrogation, a minimum of food and drink and some rough handling by the guards. He said the by the time he took part in the final demonstration, he had reached the stage when he had to convince himself that it was only simulated.

That afternoon we left Bad Tolz and made our way to Munich by train. As we had been booked to travel to the Hook of Holland the following day, some of the American officers with whom we'd got friendly during the course, suggested we stay the night with them at their Officers' Club and celebrate – it was an offer we couldn't refuse! After obtaining rooms and making ourselves presentable, we went to the dining room where we gorged ourselves – to make up for the weight we'd lost during our treks around Bavaria. Replete, we then piled into a taxi and set off on a tour of the city – the game was on!

Our first stop was at the Hoffbrauhaus where Hitler held some of his Party meetings in the thirties. There we sampled the renowned Bavarian beer from litre steins brought to us by muscular bar waitresses, carrying three steins in each hand, while we were entertained by an Oompah band. After slaking our thirst, we went to the city square to see the famous clock with its revolving figures. Then we resumed our tour of some of the other less educational venues! Led by our American guides we discovered the night life of Munich could be quite entertaining. We got back to the Officers' Club in the early hours of the morning feeling no pain whatsoever!

Our train to the Hook of Holland was scheduled to leave at a reasonable hour the following day, giving us a bit of leeway to overcome the effects of the previous night's revelry and allowed us time to bid farewell to our American comrades. Our train journey along the picturesque Rhine valley passed without incident and we arrived in good time to catch the night ferry which took us to Harwich where we disembarked and split up to return to our respective units.

When I reported to the Wing Commander Flying two days later I had to give him a full debrief. When I had done this he decided that I should give a talk to the aircrew and tell them what the dreaded Bad Tolz course entailed. A couple of days later I gave my talk and although it was well received, not one of them offered to be the next volunteer for two weeks 'holiday' in Bavaria. I can't imagine why.

While still continuing to wait for the arrival of the Valiants, we had another diversion. It was the time when the Jaguar racing car reigned supreme at Le Mans. To test the cars and equipment the Jaguar company obtained permission to use our new runway and perimeter as a test-track to prepare their cars for forthcoming races. It was quite something to watch them hurtling down the runway reaching fantastic speeds during the day and night tests. Some of us tried to scrounge rides, but had no joy, nor were there any free samples!

Eventually, at the beginning of 1955, the Valiants started to arrive and after a while the OCU began to function as planned. To begin with the noise of the four-jet aircraft especially when they operated at night caused some consternation to the civil population in the surrounding area and our new Station Commander, Group Captain B.P. Young, with whom I'd served previously[1] received some abusive correspondence. He gave me the unenviable task of drafting replies to convince them that we sympathised, but asked them to realise it was all a necessary part of protecting their freedom. Our diplomacy paid off and in a relatively short time good relations were established. The OCU got into full production and Canberra squadrons within the Group were re-equipped and manned by the newly converted aircrew from the OCU. Early in 1956, a Press presentation was held at Gaydon to publicise the Valiant and we were swamped with reporters from the National Press. It turned out that this was to pre-empt the visit to RAF Marham (one of the new Valiant stations) by Mr Kruschev, head of the Russian Politburo.

I continued in my Int/OPs post, escaping from my desk whenever I could to get airborne in the Station Flight aircraft. The Flight had acquired a T4 Canberra in which I managed to scrounge the odd trip. One such flight was memorable. It took place on one of those rare days with cloudless blue skies and limitless visibility. Our flight path took us up the middle of the country and as we flew at altitude we could see from coast to coast, observing, at the same time, both the North Sea and the Irish Sea; a wonderful sight.

In October 1956 the Suez incident took place and the OCU Valiants and crews were detailed as a back-up force to support the Valiant squadrons who were actively involved. I was given the task of producing the Operation Order by our Wing Commander Flying, W/Cdr 'Hank' Iveson (an old acquaintance) who had replaced W/Cdr Lewis Hodges. This turned out to be my last involvement with the 'V' Force, because in November I was pleased to be relieved from my Air Intelligence post and sent to fly Gloster Meteors on a jet All Weather Course.

Notes
1 See Chapter Eight.

Seventeen
Jet Flying

I reported to No. 4 Flying Training School at RAF Worksop and commenced the All Weather Course at the end of November 1956, where to begin with I received dual instruction on the Meteor T Mk 7 twin-jet. Apart from the odd scrounged trip in the Canberra T Mk IV at Gaydon and my quick jet conversion on the Vampire Mk V FB at CFS in 1952, this was my first serious introduction to jet flying, quite a change from flogging the Station Flight Ansons around the sky.

However, with the assistance of a considerate and forbearing flight commander (S/Ldr Jack Britten), I made satisfactory progress and was sent solo, first in the T Mk 7, then in the single-seat Mk 8. My first solo flight was a repeat of my first flight in the Vampire, the Meteor at this stage being slightly ahead of me, but I coped and graduated to the aerobatic stage. I recall one instructional aerobatic session particularly, when my instructor blithely asked me to do a 'Derry Turn' (a new aerobatic manoeuvre) invented by the De Havilland test pilot, John Derry who was unfortunately killed flying the De Havilland 110 during an air display at Farnborough in September 1952. I was completely ignorant of the manoeuvre which was basically a roll-out from a steep turn, resulting in the aircraft ending up on a flight path opposite to that at the point of entry into the turn. On discovering my ignorance, my instructor proceeded to enlighten me with a demonstration, after which he suggested I try a few myself!

As you can imagine, my first attempts were, in Service vernacular, 'shambolic'. However I was determined to prove that even if I wasn't an aerobatic ace, I would have a go at anything, so continued my attempts until he was satisfied with my progress. The Derry Turn entails enduring a certain amount of 'G' and I suspect that when my tutor suggested it was time to go home he'd had enough. I think that his motives were slightly ulterior when he suggested that I continue my efforts to improve my Derry Turn technique when I flew my solo aerobatic details!

It was during one of my solo flights carrying out high-level aerobatics in the Mk 8, that I involuntarily got my come-uppance, when I stalled at the top of a loop. After a few frightening moments, during which the aircraft seemed to hang in mid-air, the nose dropped and went through the vertical to the beginning of a 'bunt' (outside loop). When the stall had occurred I had throttled back and centralised the controls, then prayed, hoping to avoid a spin developing! Luckily it didn't and I breathed sigh of relief as the oscillations through the vertical diminished and I was able to regain control, to fly straight and level until everything, including my blood pressure, got back to normal!

I continued through the various stages of the course, including single engine (throttled

Gloster Meteor Mark T VII.

back) practice, suffering the usual knee trembling after-effects of having to lock your knee when using full rudder against the 'live' engine. After successfully completing the day flying schedule we progressed to the night flying stage – 'circuits and bumps' (dual and solo) followed by solo night exercises.

My introduction to this latter stage was a flight I'll always remember. It happened on one of those cold, dark, starlit winter nights when the air was gin clear. In the dimly-lit hangar area I carried out my outside checks, being most meticulous – I never had any ambition to be the boldest pilot in the RAF, only the oldest!

Having completed my checks I was assisted into the Meteor 8 by one of the attending ground crew, who helped me to strap in and remove the safety-pins from the 'bang' (ejection) seat. This done, I settled down and carried out my pre-starting checks, then getting clearance from the ground crew I started the engines in turn, checking the temperatures and pressures as they exploded into life. When they were both running smoothly I called Air Traffic Control, got taxi clearance, waved the chocks away, then following the directions from the torch-waving marshaller taxied out onto the lighted perimeter track. As I taxied towards the runway in use, I carried out my pre-take-off checks.

Arriving at the take-off point, I obtained take-off clearance from Traffic, turned onto the runway, lined up the Meteor on the centre-line and after a quick glance at the temperature and pressure gauges I opened up the throttles and released the brakes. As I steered the aircraft the surge of power forced me back into my seat. The runway lights passed with increasing rapidity and when take-off speed was reached I eased the Meteor off the ground and selected under-carriage up. As the runway lights quickly disappeared beneath me I transferred my concentration to flying on instruments and completed my after take-off checks. When I was satisfied everything was normal, I settled down to climb away from the airfield after getting clearance from Control.

Turning onto a north-westerly heading, I re-adjusted the aircraft trim and continued climbing. The initial adrenalin surge which accompanied every take-off eased and I settled down. The suffused glow of the instrument and cockpit lighting gave the panel an eerie appearance. Outside the cockpit stars twinkled in the inky darkness above and the lights of the towns below sparkled like jewels thrown haphazardly on black velvet. There was no sound in the cockpit except for my regulated breathing in the oxygen mask and as I hurtled upwards it felt as if I was suspended in space.

A crackling transmission on the R/T from another aircraft brought me out of my reverie. I scanned the instruments and noted I was approaching the altitude for the first part of the exercise. I levelled the Meteor at 38,000 feet, retrimmed, carried out the relevant checks, then turned onto a course to head back towards base on a 'High Speed' run, i.e. up to limiting Mach number (the speed at which the initial effects of approaching the speed of sound become evident).

When settled on course I advanced the throttles progressively to fully open. I had carried out this exercise during day flying so I thought I knew what to expect, but I found it was very different hurtling through the inky blackness with no external reference and having to concentrate on the flying instruments alone and disregard the misleading physical sensations.

As the speed increased, so did the adrenalin flow when I felt the onset of compressibility. The nose of the aircraft yawed from side to side and pitched up and down. A quick check of the Mach meter indicated I was reaching the limit and time to initiate recovery action. I throttled back the engines and extended the airbrakes. The speed decreased, the pitching and yawing subsided and I was able to regain full control of the aircraft and my composure. When I had everything on an even keel, I turned the Meteor onto a reciprocal course and repeated the 'High Speed' sequence. This time I was more composed and able to enjoy it and ignore the physical sensations.

It was now time for the next part of the exercise – a maximum rate (4,000 feet a minute plus) descent from my present altitude of 38,000 feet down to 22,000 feet at a constant Mach

Gloster Meteor Mark F8.

indication. I set the throttles and eased the aircraft into the descent attitude. The speed quickly built up and as the Meteor hurtled earthwards I had once again to concentrate on primary flying instruments and ignore the physical sensation that this time the aircraft was pitching tail over nose into a 'bunt' (outside loop). The Artificial Horizon toppled, the Altimeter unwound at an alarming rate and the pointer of the VSI (Vertical Speed Indicator) was hard against the stops, however I maintained my concentration and kept everything under control.

When I was approaching 24,000 feet, I commenced recovery to level out and it wasn't long until I was flying straight and level at 22,000 feet at normal cruising speed. I checked my fuel remaining and requested a QGH (radio-controlled homing and descent through cloud). They came back loud and clear and I commenced the descent procedure. The weather was still quite clear, but there seemed to be a mist forming at the lower levels.

I continued descending under radio control for a straight-in approach and it wasn't long before the runway lights were visible. Control got me onto the final approach path and gave me permission to land visually, so I continued down the slope. I was coming in nicely at a steady rate of descent and on the centre-line of the lighted runway, when suddenly without warning, all the runway lights disappeared!

By this time I was down to 500 feet, the situation was fraught to say the least, but there was only one course of action, I whanged open the throttles, retracted the undercarriage and flaps and climbed straight ahead on instruments, because I couldn't see out of the canopy. As I did so I realised why the airfield lights had disappeared – the aircraft canopy had iced-up! The aircraft having been flying at and descending from 38,000 feet where the outside air temperature was between minus 40 to 50 degrees, was still ice-cold and when it came into the warmer moist air at the lower level, it had iced-up. I called Air Traffic Control and warned them of my predicament. They came back immediately and instructed me to fly around at high speed to burn off the ice. I opened the throttles and started to circle the field and the speed built up, but by this time my fuel stocks were getting perilously low. I had my eyes glued to the fuel gauges and the pointers were hovering around the zero mark. I fervently hoped the ice would disperse quickly as I didn't relish the prospect of either 'banging out' (ejecting) or crash-landing in the dark! Fortunately the ice melted quickly from the canopy, allowing me to see the airfield lights. Thankfully I re-oriented myself, turned the aircraft onto finals and informed Air Traffic I was coming straight in. During those last few hundred feet I didn't look at the fuel gauges and as the ground got close I literally threw the Meteor onto the tarmac. Rolling to the first intersection I turned off the runway and returned to the parking area, reflecting that this was one night flight (fright) I'd always remember! The ground crew told me later that they dipped the tanks prior to refuelling and couldn't get a reading!

Shortly afterwards I passed my Instrument Rating Test and completed the course. Let's face it after my exciting night flying session, I had no trouble concentrating on my instruments!

I returned to RAF Gaydon to await developments and in June 1957 I was posted to the Bombing School at RAF Lindholme on a pilots' bombing course to bring me up to date with the latest bombing techniques, after which I was posted to RAF Bassingbourne at the beginning of July '57 to convert onto Canberras.

After dual instruction on the Canberra T Mk IV, I soloed and commenced flying the B Mk 2, the two crew version. I progressed through the various stages of day and night

English Electric Canberra, Mark B2.

training. My first day solo cross-country went according to plan except far a little hiccup which occurred on the last leg. We were flying in the region of 40,000 feet and Bob Bowler my Nav/Bomb-aimer went up front to set up the bomb-sight for the bombing detail at the end of the exercise. He had no sooner got there when the Pressurisation Failure Warning horn blared in our headsets, indicating the possibility of an explosive decompression. I immediately went onto 100% oxygen and warned Bob to do the same, while I stuffed the nose down to lose altitude and assess the situation. The possible decompression fortunately didn't occur and after carrying out checks we came to the conclusion the warning was spurious and were able to complete the exercise as planned.

Later during the course we were involved in a more pleasant and spectacular one-off exercise when we took part in the annual Air Show at Farnborough along with Valiants of the 'V' Force. It took the form of the Valiants flying over Farnborough at contrail level, making trails, followed by our Canberras, also trailing, but on a 90 degree intercept. The result was a 'lattice' of contrails over the top of Farnborough, which was apparently spectacular when viewed from the ground.

I was about to complete the course when disaster struck – I developed a medical problem which affected my ability to continue flying Canberras. I was taken off flying and grounded. The unfortunate outcome was that instead of finishing the course and being posted to a Canberra squadron as I had hoped, I was posted at the end of 1957 back to the Bombing School at RAF Lindholme as Intelligence Security Officer.

Eighteen
Serving On The Ground and In The Air

It was at the beginning of 1958, when I took over as Intelligence/Security Officer at RAF Lindholme, where I'd been recently on the Bombing Course. I found my duties also included being Officer I/C the RAF Police, so once I settled in, I established liaison with the local Civil Police in my normal security role and with the Special Branch in my Air Intelligence/Security role. I was kept busy in both roles but after a couple of months when the medics declared me fit to resume flying, I got airborne in the Station Flight Anson whenever I could.

However these activities were interrupted in May 1958, when I was sent off at very short notice to Cyprus, as a member of an air operations planning team to implement contingency plans to counter a threatened outbreak of hostilities in the Middle East. Our planning team, comprising representatives from Fighter, Bomber and Coastal Commands was flown to Cyprus by Comet aircraft, where we set up shop at the Air Headquarters at RAF Espiskopi and got cracking. The crisis came to a head when a group of Iraqi Army officers inspired by Colonel Nasser of Egypt, carried out a coup which destroyed the pro-western regime. Iraq's King Feisal, Crown Prince Abdullah and General Nuri Said, the Prime Minister were assassinated. This put pressure on Jordan and the Lebanon, who appealed to Britain and America for assistance. King Hussein of Jordan complained that Syrian troops were massing to attack. On the 15 July the US 6th Fleet landed 1,700 marines at Beirut and two days later RAF Beverley and Hastings aircraft of Transport Command landed 2,000 paratroops at Amman. British troops were also flown in from Kenya to Bahrein as a 'fire-brigade' force in the event of trouble in the Persian Gulf. Other British units were sent to Malta and Cyprus. This quick action by Britain and America nipped the plot in the bud and the tension eased.

Because of the limited living accommodation at RAF Episkopi, our Planning Team had to live in frontier tents, small square-shaped, half-walled buildings with tented roofs. Although they and the facilities were a bit primitive, the weather was warm and sunny and our tents were sited on a cliff overlooking Episkopi Bay, so during our off-duty periods we were able to swim in the Bay (there was no sign of Aphrodite!) and sunbathe on the beach. Thankfully the crisis was averted and after a couple of months on standby we were stood down. I returned to the UK at RAF Lindholme and resumed my normal duties.

In post-war years a number of selected RAF stations were opened to the public annually during September to commemorate the Battle of Britain and RAF Lindholme was one of these with a static and flying display laid on. I was involved as the member of the planning committee to co-ordinate security arrangements. Also, it was the custom to invite a celebrity to open the proceedings and on one occasion I was given the additional task of escorting officer. I had always been a keen cricketer and it made my day when I had the privilege of meeting and escorting the famous English Test Captain and Yorkshire cricketer, Sir Leonard Hutton, and his Lady.

I continued at Lindholme until February 1960, when I was informed that I was to be posted to RAF Mildenhall to take over as Officer Commanding Headquarters No. 3 Group, Bomber Command, Communications Flight. Prior to reporting to Mildenhall, I went to the Bomber Command Communications Squadron where I renewed my Flying Instructors' Rating and qualified as Instrument Rating Examiner.

On my arrival at No. 3 Group Headquarters to take up my new post, I reported to the SASO (Senior Air Staff Officer) Air Commodore W. Coles DSO DFC AFC, (later Air Marshal Sir W. Coles KBE CB DSO DFC AFC). I had met him previously in his capacity as Assistant Commandant at the Central Flying Instructors' School, RAF Little Rissington, when I first qualified as an instructor.

He put me in the picture and outlined my duties as OC Communications Flight. He explained that RAF Mildenhall was occupied by the American Air Force and it was the chief air terminal (staging post) in Europe for their Air Transport Service. They were responsible for operating and maintaining all the airfield facilities – Air Traffic Control, Meteorological and Crash Services etc. The No. 3 Group Headquarters and Communications Flight were the only RAF elements on the base. It would therefore be my responsibility to maintain close liaison and co-ordinate all our flying activities with our American counterparts.

My specific flying duties would be to fly the Air Officer Commanding, Air Vice-Marshal M.H. Dwyer CB CBE and his staff on their various inspection and liaison visits (a member of his staff at this time was W/Cdr M.J. Beetham DFC AFC, later Marshal of the RAF, Chief of the Air Staff).

I was also responsible for organising a continuation flying training programme to enable GD (flying) Staff Officers to keep their hands in. Another commitment was checking out and instrument rating pilots on the stations in our group who flew Station Communications aircraft.

The Headquarters Communications aircraft comprised two Ansons in the VIP role, another Anson in the multi-passenger and training roles and two Chipmunks in the single-passenger and training roles. The Communications Flight personnel establishment was one GD Officer (pilot), one GD Officer (Navigator) one Flight Sergeant (Fitter IIE), one Sergeant (Fitter IIA), two Corporals and approximately twenty-five airmen of various trades.

I recall my first flight was to fly the AOC (whom I'd met previously when he was Group Captain Station Commander at Fayid during my Suez Canal Zone tour) and his senior staff officers to RAF Lindholme to attend a celebration for the success of the Bomber Command 'V' Force Bombing team, during the USAF SAC (Strategic Air Command)/ RAF Bombing Competition in America.

De Havilland Chipmunk.

Avro Anson.

The ADC (aide-de-camp) to the AOC sat up front with me and acted as my navigator and the flight to Lindholme passed without incident. It was late that night when the celebrations finished and we took off on the return flight. Mildenhall at that time was unfit for night landings due to work in progress on the airfield lighting, so I had arranged for us to land at the nearby USAF Fighter base at Lakenheath. The flight proceeded as planned until we were carrying out our landing at Lakenheath. We were on our final approach when there was a power failure and the airfield blacked out temporarily (shades of my Meteor night flying episode). However, with the aid of my landing-light I was able to see the runway and land safely – my luck must have been in because I put the Anson down as smoothly as a cat peeing on velvet! When the ADC informed the AOC what had happened, I got a verbal pat on the back from him.

I soon discovered that as well as normal communications flights, I was given other and sometimes unusual flying 'training' flights. The volume and regularity of these 'training' sorties seemed to be influenced by how well the salmon were running in Scotland, or when vital items of 'defence' equipment were required by RAF stations located in the vicinity of venues where sporting events of national importance took place.

One of the mast bizarre tasks I was given happened shortly after I'd taken over the flight. The ADC to the AOC telephoned me one morning to tell me I was required to transport three live geese to a RAF Station up north. My first reaction was to check the date – no, it wasn't April 1st, so he must be serious. My next question was, 'Why?' Was it because they were running short of rations up north, or were they going to use the geese in the security role – emulating the Romans when the Gauls invaded Rome! It turned out it was a goodwill gesture! However mine was not to reason why, and I prepared accordingly. I called in the 'Chiefy', put him in the picture and asked him to detail two of our airmen to 'volunteer' to be goose-herds for the flight. When they appeared I briefed them and advised them to arm themselves with a heavy spanner, or some such blunt instrument to deal with the geese if they got loose in the aircraft – imagine the mayhem if they did!

The geese were eventually delivered to me, tied in sacks with their heads protruding from the tops, and the goose-herds got them aboard the aircraft, carefully keeping out of range of their beaks. Thankfully nothing untoward happened during the flight and we delivered the geese to their destination to serve whatever purpose they were destined for. On the return flight one of our droll goose-herds observed that he got the impression his charges had been a bit 'hissed off'!

On another occasion I was given a more sombre task. An ex-wartime aircrew officer died at a nearby RAF station and it was discovered that he had requested in his will that, after cremation, his ashes be scattered over the North Sea, fifty miles off the Norfolk coast. The officer's family's appeal to Air Ministry was granted and I was given the task.

I liaised with the RAF padre at the Station where the officer had served and he advised me he would be coming with me on the flight and that he would conduct a short service when he scattered the ashes. On the day selected he reported to me and I briefed him on the procedure we would carry out. The fuselage door had been removed from the aircraft I intended to use and temporary safety harnesses fitted. On arrival at the dropping zone he and my navigator Ron Bicknell would go to the door aperture through which the ashes were to be scattered. I was most particular to advise him to make sure the urn was well out through the door before he removed the lid.

We took off and flew to the dropping area, where the padre and Ron went to the rear fuselage to carry out the task. About ten minutes later they came back to the cockpit. The padre was slightly ashen and shame-faced – Ron was just hacked off. The obvious had happened – the padre had removed the lid from the urn before it was well through the door aperture and the slipstream had sucked the ashes from the urn – some of which had come back over the two mourners, much to their embarrassment and discomfort. The padre didn't stay for the 'debriefing' when we landed!

After I'd been at Mildenhall for about eighteen months both the incumbent AOC and SASO were posted. The AOC's replacement was Air Vice-Marshal B.K. Burnett DFC AFC BA with whom I had served when he was Station Commander at RAF Gaydon. The post of SASO was taken over by Air Commodore J.E. 'Johnnie' Johnson DSO★★ DFC★ (later Air Vice-Marshal CB CBE DSO★★ DFC★) the RAF's top-scoring fighter ace during the Second World War (and very keen salmon fisherman), who I had also known previously.

Not long after he had taken over, I flew the new AOC to Wisley, where he was met by an ex-Air Marshal now a 'big noise' in aircraft industry, who took him to Brooklands for a presentation on the prototype of the TSR2, which was envisaged as the next combat aircraft replacement for the RAF. Before they left for Brooklands, the Air Marshal arranged for one of the company pilots to look after me and my navigator, who was now Flight Lieutenant Ron Stevens. Our escort took us to the company canteen for lunch and while we waited and were chatting, I felt a tap on my shoulder. Turning, I discovered an old acquaintance, 'Mac' Macnamara, a pilot with whom I'd flown on York's during my long-range transport days. During our subsequent chat, he told me after our York days he had taken the Course at the Empire Test Pilots School, He had then left the RAF joined Vickers and was now the company's No. 2 test pilot on the VC10. After catching up on our news, he asked me what I was doing at Wisley. When I told him I'd brought our AOC for a presentation on the TSR2, he said,'He'll be at Brooklands all afternoon, so if you like, after we have lunch I will give you a 'presentation' on the No. 2 prototype VC10 which I'm going to fly to Aden for tropical trials.' Naturally, I jumped at the chance and after lunch, we went to the VC10 where I spent one of the most enjoyable and informative sessions in my flying career. The VC10 is still a wonderful aircraft, and still in service with the RAF. At that time, it was, in my humble opinion, a better civil transport aircraft than its American Boeing rival. Unfortunately the British aircraft industry didn't have the sales know-how and financial clout that the Americans had, to make it a world-wide success.

When the AOC came back to Wisley, we prepared to return to Mildenhall. Usually he sat in his seat in the fuselage but that day he elected to sit up front in the second pilot's seat. After we had taken off and set course he asked me if the Company had looked after us. When I told him what had happened he was most interested and then proceeded to give me a run-down on the presentation he'd been given on the TSR2. From what he told me I gathered he was looking forward enthusiastically to it being adopted by the RAF. It is again in my humble opinion, a tragedy that the government of the day turned it down. Grave damage was done to the British aircraft industry and the RAF when they cancelled it, destroyed the two prototypes, the plans, drawings, jigs and tools and dispersed a skilled works team. Not only did this cost the country millions of pounds in penalties when they cancelled its replacement, the American F111 which failed to meet RAF operational requirements, but also left the RAF without a suitable modern combat aircraft.

One of the most worthwhile commitments I had with the Comm. Flight occurred annually when we participated in the American Memorial Service held at the American War Graves Cemetery at Madingley, near Cambridge, where 3,808 American servicemen are buried, mostly flying personnel, casualties of the air war over Europe during the Second World War.

I was involved with the RAF participation in the ceremony by carrying out a low fly-past in one of my Ansons over the cemetery during which two of my airmen scattered 3,808 sweet peas over the graves from the rear-door aperture of the aircraft. A fitting tribute and gesture of remembrance from the RAF for the sacrifice by our wartime American comrades.

Not far from RAF Mildenhall, is the little village of Worlington, where at that time there was a country club, owned and run by John Lankester Parker[1] known as Jack, who kindly offered the privilege of honorary membership to our Officers' Mess members. Jack Lankester Parker was an ex-aviator of note. He had been the Chief Test Pilot for Short Brothers before he retired.

During one of my visits to his club when he discovered I'd done a tour on Sunderland flying-boats during the war we became kindred spirits. He told me during subsequent conversations of some of the highlights of his exciting and interesting career. He was born in 1896 and after surviving a very serious illness during his early life, he became a pilot and

Dropping flowers over American USAF graves in Madingley Cemetery.

subsequently a test pilot with Short Brothers, testing a series of flying boats pre-Second World War, including the Sunderland and the 'C' class Empire flying-boats of Britain's Imperial Airways.

In 1938 he was involved with the Short-Mayo Composite experiments with a 'C' type flying-boat, christened 'Maia', with 'Mercury' a twin-float, four-engined aircraft mounted on a frame above the centre of the wing of Maia. Jack flew Maia while Don Bennett (later Air Vice-Marshal CB CBE DSO) flew Mercury. Operationally, Maia served to lift Mercury to cruising altitude, when they separated, allowing Mercury to proceed to its destination fully laden. On 21 July 1938, a first flight was made non-stop from Foynes, Ireland, to Montreal, Canada, and a second flight made on the 6 October 1938 from Dundee to South Africa (6,044 miles) – an international record for seaplanes. Although this 'pick-a-back' system was thought to be practical for the transport of high priority cargo and mail, it was discontinued when war broke out and when in-flight refuelling became a more practical proposition.

With the outbreak of war, Jack continued flight tests and experiments with the Sunderland, and also with the development of the Short Stirling, which was the RAF's first four-engined bomber. He told me the first prototype Stirling he tested was a half-scale model, powered by four Pobjoy engines and that the cockpit was just big enough for himself, the flying controls and the aircraft instruments. He also told me of other experiments with the Sunderland, one of them being trials to test the feasibility of transporting a midget-submarine to drop within range of targets in enemy and occupied ports.

We had some wonderfully interesting conversations and it was a privilege to have known him. Although at this time he was getting on in years he was Chairman of GAPAN (Guild of Air Pilots and Navigators) and still interested and abreast of all that was happening in the world of aviation – a great and unforgettable character.

He stimulated my interest to the extent that I obtained my private pilots' licence, my civil flying instructors' endorsement and my Certificate of Appointment as Royal Aero Club Official Observer (for observing practical flying tests and examining applicants for Private Pilots' Licences), which I was able to put to good use while I was at Mildenhall.

Our American friends at Mildenhall ran a 'Dependents' Flying Club, for the benefit of any of their personnel who wished to fly as a hobby. During one of our exchange 'bun-fights' (Mess Dining-in Nights) I asked one of my American flying acquaintances whether it would be possible for me to fly with the club during my off-duty hours. He said he would make enquiries for me and a few days later, the Base Commander contacted me to say he had no objection, as long as I also got RAF permission. So I applied 'through the proper channels' and was granted permission by the AOC.

Subsequently I joined the club, was checked out on their three single-engined light aircraft, the Aeronca, the Tri-pacer and the Cessna 120 having the time of my life. Also when the American officer I/C the club learned that I held a UK Instructors' civil licence, he got permission to co-opt me into his instructional team.

The Tri-pacer and the Cessna 120 were well equipped and a pleasure to fly, but the Aeronca was a real basic aeroplane. It was a two-seat tandem and our model was equipped with dual primary flying controls but it had no flight or engine instruments in the rear cockpit, so instructing could be interesting, especially during take-offs and landings if the student in the front was above average physique, thus obstructing the view of the ASI and other instruments. Despite this small drawback it was fairly easy to fly and its landing speed was very slow.

My tour at Mildenhall was extended until the middle of 1963, when I was posted to do a ground school refresher course on Valettas, before going to RAF Hullavington to do the flying refresher. This was in preparation before proceeding overseas to Aden to take over the Communications Squadron. I successfully completed the ground course but on reporting to Hullavington I was informed that due to cuts in the Defence budget, the Communications Squadron at Aden was being disbanded and my Valetta course was cancelled – so there I was 'raring', but with nowhere to go'!

However, all was not lost. Eventually things were sorted out and in November I was posted to convert onto the four-engined turbo-prop Argosy. After converting I was to proceed to RAF Khormaksar (Aden) to join No. 105 Argosy Squadron.

Notes

1 J.L. Parker OBE FRAeS Hon MSLAET. Instructor Seaplane School, Windermere 1915-16. Test Pilot Prodger-Isaac Aviation Co. 1916-18, Chief Test Pilot at Shorts 1916-45.

Aeronca.

Cessna 120.

Tri-pacer.

Nineteen

Swansong In Aden

At the end of October 1963, I was posted to 242 OCU to convert onto the Argosy. The first part of the conversion was a detachment to the Hawker Siddeley Aircraft works at Coventry to learn all there was to know about the Argosy electrics and airframe. It proved to be an interesting and comprehensive learning period.

The Argosy was originally designed by the former Armstrong Whitworth Aircraft Company in 1950 to meet the requirement for a large freight carrying aircraft for the civil air freight market. It was a twin-boom, four-engine, aircraft with a 'roll on roll off' capacity for easy loading and off-loading and quick turn around operation. It had a two-pilot crew.

Unfortunately it was not taken up in any great numbers by the civil aircraft operators, despite the fact that two American firms who bought them achieved a very high utility rate. So presumably for political reasons it was passed on to the Ministry of Defence.

To meet all the joint service operational requirements, the fuselage was re-designed with upward and downward hinging rear loading doors which could be opened in flight for air operations. The nose door was deleted, the floor was strengthened to support the weight of either a Ferret Scout Car, a Saracen Armoured Car or 'Boscombe Down' Platforms (pallets containing military supplies). It could also be used in the Paratroop, Army Support and Medical Casevac roles. To enable it to also operate in the Passenger/Freight role, the crew complement was increased to two pilots, a navigator, a flight engineer, a wireless operator and an air-quartermaster. A sophisticated flight system linked to the automatic pilot and radio was installed together with navigational radar, VHF, UHF and H/F communications radio, weather warning radar and an audio and visual emergency warning system.

It was powered by four 2,680hp Rolls Royce Dart 101 turbo-prop engines and was fitted with nose-wheel (tiller) steering and stall-warning stick-shakers. According to published details, it was supposed to be capable of a cruising speed of 269mph at 20,000 feet, a service ceiling of 25,000 feet, a maximum range of 3,280 miles and carrying the following loads: One 105mm Pack Howitzer, a Ferret Scout Car and Wombat anti-tank gun or a Saracen armoured car. Alternatively fifty-four paratroops, sixty-nine fully equipped soldiers or forty-eight stretchers. I doubt whether these figures were ever achieved and in reality the Argosy turned out to be a jack of all trades transport aircraft but master of none. It was under-powered with the Dart 101 engines and only a slight improvement was achieved when it was fitted with the up-graded Dart 102 engines. Another case of the political tail wagging the operational dog!

Hawker Siddeley Argosy.

After completing the Electrics and Airframe Course at Coventry, I returned to RAF Thorney Island for the flying. Up to then my actual pilot time on four-engined aircraft had been the few unofficial hours I'd scrounged during the war on Bomber and Coastal Command aircraft and on Yorks immediately after the war, so flying the modern Argosy was a new experience. It was quite a jump from flying the old twin-engine Anson and it took me sometime to assimilate the new procedures and to get used to handling the new equipment. I spent hours poring over flight planning data and in the Flight Simulator during which it was possible to simulate actual route trips and practice every possible emergency. However I struggled through it and completed all the exercises including Army Support, dropping paratroops, supplies and the Boscombe Down Platforms. The latter exercise was, to put it mildly, hair-raising. Two platforms (pallets), each weighing 8,000 lbs, linked together were dropped in tandem from a fairly low altitude. Parachutes attached to the first platform deployed pulling it through the rear-hinged doors. As it cleared the aircraft it pulled the attached second platform after it. The nose-up change in trim as they left the aircraft was considerable especially when the second one shot from the front of the fuselage through the rear doors. Even with maximum forward pressure on the stick it was difficult to maintain any semblance of control and the stall-warning 'stick-shakers' worked overtime – a sobering experience and afterwards I remember thinking that it might be rather hazardous if we ever had to do it for real, in combat conditions!

All the day flying on the course took place from Thorney Island, but when we got to the night flying stage we were sent on detachment to Tripoli to fly from there. The reason for this was apparently because some influential residents in the Thorney Island vicinity were allergic to night flying! However, the weather in Tripoli was nice and warm, the beer was cold and we were able to complete our night flying, so why worry? On return to Thorney Island we awaited our postings and when they came through I discovered I was

Larry Donnelly at RAF Khormaksar 1965.

to join the Argosy squadron, No. 105 based at Khormaksar, Aden, as planned originally.

After embarkation leave, I reported to RAF Lyneham, from where I flew in a Transport Command Britannia to Khormaksar. It was May 1964, the hot season was well under way and the temperature when we landed there was in the nineties.

Once settled in on the squadron I commenced flying the various routes. The round the houses run was to Bahrein via Riyan, Salala, Masirah Island, and Sharjah. Some of these outposts of the Empire had short natural surface landing strips, so tyre wear was considerable. The use of the strips was under lease from the local Sultans/Sheikhs one of whom insisted that the rent be paid annually in Marie Therese silver dollars, which he apparently kept in large trunks in his sleeping quarters! There was also the Bahrein overflight, which was a non-stop flight to Bahrein across the Arabian desert, then a quick turn-round back to Khormaksar. The reason for this was that the diplomatic clearance issued by the Saudi authorities only lasted for twenty-four hours and you had to reapply if it expired for any reason. Flying over the desert at 12,000 feet during the day, it looked like 'moon country', completely uninhabited, however the return flight during the hours of darkness revealed fires from the Bedouin camps dotted all along the route.

Our other scheduled routes were to Eastleigh (Nairobi), Salisbury (Zimbabwe) and Matsapa (Swaziland). Operating in and out of the high altitude natural surface (Murram) strip at Eastleigh could present problems especially during the wet season. If the Eastleigh strip was unusable for a loaded Argosy it had to be flown empty to Nairobi International Airport with its 3,000 yards plus concrete runway and the load transported by road from Eastleigh to Nairobi – another example of the Argosy operating and weight carrying limitations. We were well and truly WAT (Weight, Altitude and Temperature) limited, in fact it was rumoured that on one occasion the air quartermaster risked being court-martialled for leaving the payload under the crew-room table!

I flew with the squadron until the beginning of 1965, when I unfortunately failed the flying medical requirements. The outcome was that I was flown back to the UK to Wroughton RAF hospital where I was subjected to intensive examinations, during which it was discovered I had permanent middle ear damage which adversely affected my balance and hearing. I was then passed onto the Central Medical Board in London, where I was told that I was grounded, but I could return to Khormaksar and finish my tour in a ground capacity if a post was available. Also, after finishing my tour I was to attend another board to assess my medical condition and future career in the Service.

I returned to Khormaksar and to say I was in a state of deep depression couldn't really describe what I felt. However, the people pushers at Air Headquarters decided that that I could fill an operations planning post at Khormaksar for the rest of my tour. So I had to accept my fate and make the best of it, but after flying for nearly twenty-eight years, it was a bitter pill to swallow. I served the rest of my tour as a mahogany bomber pilot, something I'd always attempted to avoid. However, the planning post had its moments, one of my tasks was to review and up-date the operational contingency plans for the evacuation of civilians and servicemen throughout the Middle East if and when required. Possibly my handiwork was used when all the evacuations took place later. I was also given the interesting task of RAF Liaison Officer to the American Air Force Emergency Rescue Teams who were based at Khormaksar whenever NASA's Gemini orbital operations took place.

During that time I suffered another medical hiccup and spent some time in hospital, but I was able to finish my tour and return to the UK in May 1966. What with one thing and another (by this time the local security situation in Aden had deteriorated and sniper and grenade attacks were taking place against British servicemen and their families) plus my personal medical problem, I was glad to leave.

I returned to the UK where I was subjected to further medical checks at the RAF hospital at Cosford. These resulted in another appearance at CMB (Central Medical Board) who delivered their bombshell. It was decided that I was not only unfit for flying as pilot, but also unfit for further service in the RAF in any capacity!

I was sent to RAF Shawbury where I filled a supernumerary planning post until that fateful day in December 1966, when I was officially invalided out of the Service in which I'd served and flown for nearly twenty-nine, eventful years.

Epilogue

During the three month interim period between my final CMB and the fateful day of my discharge from the RAF, I returned to RAF Shawbury, to attempt to reconcile myself to my fate and plan my future. Although I was now medically unfit for flying, I wasn't, I hoped, ready for the scrap heap, because I still had to earn a living. My Civil Air Licences were now invalid because of my failure to maintain the flying medical category, so I would have to accept some sort of ground job.

I went to Aston University and participated in the Rehabilitation Course sponsored by the RAF for the benefit of officers leaving the Service. However, after the course I came to the conclusion that instead of attempting a career in a new field, I should investigate the possibility of staying in aviation and obtaining employment in the aircraft industry where my previous experience could be utilised. I wanted to stay where my abiding interest was – with aeroplanes.

So I compiled a curriculum vitae and sent copies of it with covering letters to all the prominent aircraft firms. I struck lucky and was invited to attend an interview at the Hawker Siddeley aircraft works at Hatfield, during which they offered to employ me as a technical author in their technical publications (Pilots' Manuals) department.

I accepted their offer and commenced my new career at the beginning of 1967, initially amending and up-dating the De Havilland Comet manuals. After that I graduated to the Trident IIE manuals. At this time they were upgrading the Autoland System fitted to the IIE and I became involved in writing the operational procedure.

Although my medical category precluded me from flying as pilot, it did not prevent me from flying as passenger/observer, so I was able to fly to Bedford, the civil aviation experimental airfield with De Havilland's chief test pilot, Gp Capt John Cunningham CBE DSO★ DFC★ AE, the legendary night fighter ace of the Second World War and his deputy Jimmy Phillips, where they checked out the modified Autoland procedure I'd helped to write.

I enjoyed being at Hatfield but in 1969, I was approached by BAC (British Aircraft Corporation) at Warton to join their technical publications department and become one of the team whose task was to write the manuals for the prototype of the new Anglo/French ground attack aircraft, the Jaguar. It was an offer I couldn't refuse.

I joined them and had the enjoyable task of helping to produce the manuals for the benefit of the RAF through RDT (MOD/AIR) and the French Air Force. One very pleasant part of this task involved liaison visits to Paris to consult with our opposite numbers of Breguet Aircraft Company and representatives of the French Air Force.

After the Jaguar, the follow-up project was to write the pilots' manuals for the new Multi-role Combat Aircraft (which later became known as the Tornado) which was a joint British, German and Italian venture. Everything went smoothly for me until 1975 when my health broke down, After hospitalisation and convalescence, I reluctantly had to give up my job at BAC and left the area.

However, after a while I fought my way back to a semblance of fitness and got the urge to get back into action again. In the area I was now living there were no suitable aviation type employment situations available, so I looked further afield.

Eventually I joined a large helicopter firm at Dyce (Aberdeen) airport, servicing North Sea oil rigs, as one of their Operations Co-ordinators. This turned out to be a stimulating and exciting job, though fairly stressful at times, but with the help of medication I coped. One of my most gratifying tasks was to fly out to the various oil rigs in the North Sea to check their facilities.

I continued in this capacity until the end of 1980, when I was advised by the Company Doctor that my health was once again on the blink and I should consider early retirement. Reluctantly I took his advice and retired in 1981.

At first it was difficult to settle down, but I worked at it and I'm glad I took the doctor's advice, because I'm still ticking over, even if I can't operate at full revs! I'm still as enthusiastic about flying and anything connected with it as I was when I was a 'fledgling'. I research and scribble and attend Service reunions whenever I can. I live near a RAF Station and whenever the Tornados and Jaguars screech overhead, I get a very nostalgic buzz!

Once you've been bitten by the flying bug it never leaves you. I may not have been the most brilliant pilot – as the Americans put it, I was just an average Joe – but I did succeed in fulfilling my 'quest' for wings and, in the process, I enjoyed every minute of it.

RAF Pilots' Wings.

General Index

Index of Personnel

RCAF:
    Canavan, Sgt P. 92
    Demone H. 66
    McLean, F/O 92
    Moule, Sgt R. 46, 48, 51
    Robinson, F/O 90

Royal Navy:
    Bickford Jnr, Lt R. 50
    Kerrans, Commander 113
    Walker, Capt F.J. 82-3

Index of Aircraft and Shipping

Acknowledgements

I wish to gratefully acknowledge the assistance given directly or indirectly by: Betty Baveystock, Richard Bickford Jnr, Chaz Bowyer (for his photographs), John Dawkins (for his photographs), Maureen Lakey, Malcolm Lucas (Whitley contemporary), Pete Jensen (Sunderland crewmate), Dudley Marrows (Sunderland skipper), Jock Rolland (Sunderland crewmate), Jill and Peter Rutter for their special assistance, The Royal Air Force Museum, and my dear wife for her tolerance of the hours I spent in the 'inner sanctum'.

Bibliography

Wings of War, Laddie Lucas, 1983, Huthinson & Co (Publications) Ltd
The Whitley File, Air Britain (Historians) Ltd, 1986
Halifax Special, Bruce Robertson, 1990, Ian Allan Ltd
From Hull, Hell and Halifax, Chris Planchett, 1992, Midland Counties
Flying Porcupines, Maureen Lakey
The Baveystock Papers
The Bickford Papers
The Jensen Papers